# LEARNING TO LOVE
# THE ONE YOU MARRY

# LEARNING
# TO LOVE
# THE ONE
# YOU MARRY

Advice to Young Couples About...
Commitment
Intimacy
Sex
Money
Work
And Much More

# Gary Kinnaman
Illustrations by Rob Osborne

SERVANT PUBLICATIONS
ANN ARBOR, MICHIGAN

OTHER BOOKS BY GARY C. KINNAMAN
*My Companion Through Grief*
*Angels Dark and Light*
*And These Signs Shall Follow*
*Overcoming the Dominion of Darkness*

© 1997 by Gary Kinnaman
All rights reserved.

Vine Books is an imprint of Servant Publications especially designed to serve
evangelical Christians.

All Scripture quotations, unless indicated, are taken from the HOLY BIBLE, NEW INTER-
NATIONAL VERSION®. © 1973, 1978, 1984 by International Bible Society. Used by
permission of Zondervan Publishing House. All rights reserved.

The family budget chart in chapter seven is taken from *The Financial Planning Workbook* by
Larry Burkett. © 1990 by Christian Financial Concepts, Moody Press. Used by permission.

Published by Servant Publications
P.O. Box 8617
Ann Arbor, Michigan 48107

Cover photographs: Adam Smith Prod./Westlight and Fotografia/Westlight. Used by permission.

97 98 99 00 10 9 8 7 6 5 4 3 2

Printed in the United States of America
ISBN 1-56955-011-5

LIBRARY OF CONGRESS CATALOGING-IN-PUBLICATION DATA

Kinnaman, Gary
Learning to love the one you marry : advice to young couples about— commitment, inti-
macy, sex, money, work, and much more / Gary Kinnaman ; illustrations by Rob Osborn.
    p.   cm.
ISBN 1-56955-011-5
1. Marriage—United States—Religious aspects—Christianity.   2. Married couples—United
States—Psychology.   3. Married couples—United States—Religious life.   I. Title.
BV835.K55 1997
248.8'44—dc21                                                              97-8581
                                                                             CIP

## DEDICATION

To my father and mother
Donald and Esther Kinnaman
faithful to God
and
to one another
for fifty years

# CONTENTS

## FOREWORD

I read a lot of books about marriage, and I've also written a few. That's my job. Some books I read are thought provoking. Others are somewhat interesting. But this book is outstanding. I can say without qualification, Gary's wise words to his children about marriage will be required reading for my daughters in the months leading up to or after their marriage.

When you meet Gary, as I have, it's easy to be taken with his warmth and authenticity. He's the pastor of a "mega-church" that's as warm and real as a country chapel. He has earned Master's and Doctorate degrees, and has a gift for speaking and writing that has made him a leading communicator of God's truth across our country and beyond. But that's all on his bio. What I appreciate most about Gary is what's written in the lives of his wife and children. They look and act like they're well loved. And when you talk to them, they say they live with someone who is warm and real, not plastic or pretend.

Gary comes from a long line of pastors and church leaders, and is a diligent student of God's word. But what I loved most about this book was that it carried practical words of biblical wisdom I wish I would have heard twenty years ago when Cindy and I married.

Like a lot of people today, I grew up in a single-parent home, and with no spiritual foundation. I barely knew my own father. And while my father-in-law is a wonderful man, the only advice on marriage he gave me was on our wedding day. In fact, it was just before he went to walk Cindy down the aisle. His counsel to me as I waited with the other groomsmen was: "Well, John ... if this doesn't work out, *we'll take her back!*" (Meant as a compliment to Cindy, not a cut to me ... I think!).

I longed for the kind of biblical counsel and cutting edge advice this father gives his son and daughter-in-law in *Learning to Love the One You Marry*. It's like getting to look inside a window, and see up close what a loving, Christian father would say to his children. What subjects he felt would help them most. What things they could do to draw closer to the Savior, and what issues to avoid to head off heartaches and hurt.

If you're getting married and looking for wise counsel on everything from finances to finding God's will, you've picked up the right resource. If you have a son or daughter who is getting married, they'll have a hundred "must need" things on their wedding register. But I urge you to put this book on your list of "they must have" items. It's one gift, filled with God's word and godly insight, that can help them live out a marriage as beautiful as their wedding.

John Trent, Ph.D.
Author/Speaker
President, Encouraging Words

## PREFACE

This is my fifth book, and it's as personal as any I've written. It may also be the most urgent. Marriage in America is an institution in crisis. I heard not too long ago that about half of the population of Dallas is single—not because people don't fall in love any more, but because the risks of getting married are perceived to be too high. Or people have tried marriage, and it just doesn't work.

We have become a godless nation of sand-castle families, because we are increasingly leaving God out of our social institutions, and shelving the timeless truths of his Word. And that, essentially, is what this book addresses. It's a call to come back to the basics, to bring the Bible back to a deeply spiritual generation where spirituality has no definition—and certainly no absolutes. I'm not a psychologist. I'm a husband and dad first, a pastor of a local church second, and I am a firm believer in traditional values rooted in God's Word.

People have asked me through the years, "What's special about your ministry? Why do so many people attend your church?" (We have burgeoned from a handful of people to over three thousand adults and kids every weekend.) Of course there are many reasons for a growing, vibrant church, but if I have a single passion, it's helping people reshape their lives with a biblical world view.

Let me explain. As Christian believers, we're pretty sure about what's right and wrong, moral and immoral—like adultery, murder, and abortion. And we're quick to point those things out to others. But more subtly, and perhaps even more powerfully, our faith is undermined by cultural forces. Christians are thoroughly secularized and don't know it. Yep, even real good Christians. I've seen it over and over in our church. We're more influenced by the values (or, more precisely, the values vacuum) of our culture than by what we hear in church.

You think not? Just take the simple "biblical value" of eating together (Acts 2:42-46). It builds relationships and community, right? Anyone can figure that out. But the desperation *du jour* is, "*Where's the love, man?*" Know why? Because we esteem the American "values" of convenience and privacy much more. So we don't eat together because it's not convenient, and then we wonder why we communicate with one another so poorly. We sacrifice relationships—at home and at church—on the altar of privacy.

It's just one of those little things, of course, but it's a terrible thing. Like a cancer you can't feel in your body until you find out you're dying.

This book is about seeing marriage and all of life from a counter-cultural, biblical world view. As you will find, it's full of Bible references, yet I have not taken a traditional, simplistic approach, like if wives just submit to their husbands, everything's gonna be OK. Or, the family that prays together stays together. Oh yes, I talk about those things, but in a way young couples think and feel in the dawn of a new millennium—where to them, there is no such thing as a moral absolute. I'm a flag-waver of traditional values, but in terms that non-traditionalists can understand.

So this book is offbeat and biblical at the same time. Actually, it might surprise you to know that lots of Christian books on the family are not specifically biblically-based. They are written by Christians, and they're not *unbiblical*, but many books on the Christian home are written from more of a psychological, good-common-sense perspective. Now there's not a thing wrong with that, but there's a need, a growing need, for young couples to learn more, not just about the techniques on how to make your marriage as happy as you can, but about the broader issues of life and how *everything* relates back to God.

To make the book as personal as possible, I've addressed it throughout to my son, David Kinnaman, and to his new wife, Jill. Each chapter is like a letter—sort of, but not really. And all the stories and personal anecdotes are true, about which the members of my family are mildly dismayed. They've all agreed, though, to let the book happen—for the sake of the many young couples whose marriages need as much help as we can give them.

So thank you, Marilyn (my wife of twenty-five years) for all the love in our home. And thanks, too, Shari and Matthew (our other two kids) who appear and reappear in this book. We've shared our lives with all the people in our church. Now here we go sharing them with anybody and everybody.

My thanks, too, to the people of Servant Publications. This is my third book with their company, and I am grateful for the great sense of encouragement and support I have felt from them over the last several years—especially Bert Ghezzi and Gwen Ellis, who insisted that I work even harder to make this an even better book.

I'm also indebted to a young man in our church, Rob Osborne, for all the cartoons and illustrations. I'm convinced, Rob, lots of people will buy this book just for the pictures!

## ONE

## TILL DEATH DO US PART, OR FOR AS LONG AS I'M HAPPY?

*Being faithful for a lifetime*

Jill and David, not only did you attend college in Southern California, now you get to live there! Sunshine. The beaches. Disneyland and Hollywood. The Lakers, the Dodgers, and other significant cultural opportunities.

Ten million people from every tribe and nation, nightmare traffic, smog, earthquakes. Graffiti as far as the eye can see.

And no-fault divorce.

Did you know that California became the first state to adopt "no fault" divorce, which is now the basis of law in all fifty states? According to California's 1969 Family Law Act, either partner could get out of marriage simply by citing "irreconcilable differences which have caused the irremediable breakdown of the marriage."

Since then, divorces have skyrocketed. In 1960, "only" about four hundred thousand marriages in America ended in divorce or annulment, but that number has now *tripled.* There are many reasons for this, but a recent study by the University of Oklahoma concluded that no-fault divorce laws by themselves raise the divorce rate by 15% or more.[1]

## TRAPPED IN A MISERABLE MARRIAGE

In other words, the easier you make divorce, the easier it is to divorce. Big problem, though: the aftermath of divorce is often worse than a bad marriage. Just yesterday an article in the Phoenix newspaper trumpeted: "Divorcing? This course is a must. New law requires couple to study impact on kids."

So if you ever come to the place where you think you're trapped in a miserable marriage, you've only seen the beginning of sorrows. Just get a divorce, and you will compound the suffering, for you and for everyone else in your family.

I can't imagine you guys ever getting a divorce, but then I can't imagine so many of the people in our church getting divorces, either. But they do.

Dave and Jill, it can happen to anyone, so this book is going to be in your face. Not that you've ever known me to beat around the bush. I really am sorry, Dave, for all those times I was "honest" with the family at the expense of being sensitive and kind. And I am inexpressibly grateful for the balance your gentle mother has brought to our home.

But some things just need to be said. I guess it's the preacher in me. I also want you to know what others are saying about this, like a recent study, *Marriage in America: A Report to the Nation*, prepared by the politically-diverse Council on Families in America. Interestingly, the list of prominent contributors does *not* include such notables as Billy Graham or James Dobson. No, not the name of a single, well-bred evangelical. Not a Bible-thumper among them! *But you gotta read this.* Here's an excerpt:

"America's divorce revolution has failed.

"The evidence of failure is overwhelming. The divorce revolution—by which we mean the steady displacement of a marriage culture by a culture of divorce and unwed parenthood—has created terrible hardships for children. It has burdened us with unsupportable social costs. It has failed to deliver on its promise of greater adult happiness and better relationships between men and women.

"We do not offer this assessment lightly. We recognize that these failures have been unanticipated and unintended. The divorce revolution set out to achieve some worthy goals: to foster greater equality between men and women; to improve the family lives of women; and to expand individual happiness and choice. We recognize the enduring importance of these social goals.

"Yet the divorce revolution has not brought us closer to these goals, but has cast us at a greater distance from them. Relationships between men and women are not getting better; by many measures, they are getting worse. They are becoming more difficult, fragile, and unhappy. Too many women are experiencing chronic economic insecurity. Too many men are isolated and estranged from their children. Too many people are lonely and unconnected. Too many children are angry, sad, and neglected.

"....We as a society are simply failing to teach the next generation about the meaning, purposes, and responsibilities of marriage. If this trend continues, it will constitute nothing less than an act of cultural suicide.... The most important factor of declining child well-being is the remarkable collapse of marriage, leading to growing family instability and decreasing parental investment in children.... Unless we reverse the decline of marriage, no other achievements will be powerful enough to reverse the trend of declining child well-being."[2]

## AND, SURPRISE, THE MAIN REASON
## FOR MARRIAGE IS ...

Most insightful—and chilling—is this statement from the *Report*:

"Marriage has been losing its social purpose. Instead of serving as [listen to this!] our primary institutional expression *of commitment and obligation to others, especially children,* marriage has increasingly been reduced to a vehicle—and a fragile one at that—for the emotional fulfillment of adult partners. 'Till death us do part' has been replaced by 'as long as I am happy.' Marriage is now less an institution that one belongs to and more an idea that we insist on bending to our own, quite individualistic, purposes. Fewer than 50 percent of Americans today include 'being married' as part of their definition of family values."[3]

So sad. So very sad. I think it even makes God cry. Long, long ago, God said in the Bible, "I *hate* divorce" (Malachi 2:16). I'm convinced that he hates it, not just because God is old-fashioned and religious, but because he knows what it does to people, to their children and their extended families—to whole nations.

Why do we need a report like this to bring us to our senses? Why is it so difficult for people just to take God at his word?

Not too long ago I saw a pair of cynical cartoons about love and commitment. In one, a man kneeling in a romantic pose before his lover, pleads: "I love you, Cindy. Will you marry me for a year or two?"

In another, a young child, gripping a little suitcase and standing before his startled mother, announces, "Mom, I'm leaving. I just can't make the commitment."

"NO FAULT" WEDDING PROPOSAL

### IT JUST DOESN'T RING TRUE

Well, we even have a ring for that now. Just a few months ago, I was on an airplane and read an article that told about how one London jeweler has revamped the tradition of the engagement ring to keep up with the social trend.

The ring he has designed is symbolically not quite closed.

The meaning, of course, is that you can always find a way out if things don't work out.

David and Jill, I have unwavering confidence in your faithfulness to one another, but I also know that there are a million voices out there screaming against commitment. I especially feel this in our church family, where infidelity is rampant. And I'm not just thinking about adultery.

Infidelity is about why banks fail.

It's why the government can't balance the budget, even though our nation has a multi-trillion dollar debt.

It's about credit card madness and why our nation is facing a crisis of consumer debt.

It's about people constantly changing jobs.

It's about fathers who owe thousands of dollars in child support.

It's about friends leaving our church without saying a word to Mom or me.

It's about people in the church volunteering to do something and then never showing up.

It's why people in the church commit to give to our building program and then don't give a dime.

It's about people breaking their promises more often than they keep them.

It's about me getting really depressed about all this. Sometimes it even makes me feel like saying, "The hell with my commitments, too."

No wonder people don't keep their financial commitments to the church; they can't even keep their promises to their own children!

## THE END OF THE "OLD LOYALTY"

The problem is a pervasive, cultural cancer. A couple of years ago, someone in our church who works for Motorola handed me an internal memo from George Fisher, the C.E.O. of the vast, multi-national corporation:

"In recent years," he wrote, "much has been written and major studies have been conducted that conclude that loyalty, once prized by both companies and employees, is dead.... One study just completed ... reports that instead of belonging to a group as a source of creativity and seeking ultimate harmony with the organization, today's workers are committed to their professions and the work they perform. They are referred to as 'The New Individualists'.... The 'old loyalty' is being replaced by increased employee self-interest.

"We are not ready to join the swelling ranks of U. S. executives," he avowed, "and concede that the traditional employee loyalty cannot be sustained and nurtured."

Within just a year or so of issuing this circular on loyalty, George Fisher left Motorola in a surprise move to become Chairman of Kodak.

I'm sure he had his reasons.

And so does everyone who quits a job. Sometimes it happens when one gets a divorce, too.

Think about this one. The motto for American Family Insurance is "*Loyalty*: the mark of satisfied customers." Is this *really* what loyalty means? Or is this a subtle redefinition based on changing social values? I doubt that the ad meisters ever gave it a deep thought, but the fact is that this motto remakes loyalty into something conditional, as in "*loyalty*, the mark of a satisfied employee." Or, "*loyalty*, the mark of a satisfied husband."

If you're not satisfied, if you're not happy, then don't be loyal! Get another insurance company! Quit your job! Get a different husband!

Joan Lunden's gorgeous face appears on the cover of the May, 1993, issue of *Ladies' Home Journal*, along with the caption: "I didn't leave my husband for someone else, I left for *myself*." I underscored "myself," because that's exactly the way it appears.

Yes, I'm outraged!

## TILL DEATH DO US PART

Which brings me back to the marriage vows. "For better or for worse, for richer or for poorer, in sickness and in health ... Till death us do part."

You see, marriage is about the "old loyalty," not conditional loyalty. It's about *unconditional* love and commitment, like God's love and commitment to us: "Do you think anyone is going to be able to drive a wedge between us and Christ's love for us? There is no way! Not trouble, not hard times, not hatred, not hunger, not homelessness, not bullying threats, not backstabbing, not even the worst sins listed in Scripture.... None of this fazes us because Jesus loves us. I'm absolutely convinced that nothing—nothing living or dead, angelic or demonic, today or tomorrow, high or low, thinkable or unthinkable—absolutely *nothing* can get between us and God's love because of the way that Jesus our Master has embraced us" (Romans 8:35-39, *The Message*).

Yes, the Bible allows for divorce under extraordinary circumstances, like adultery or desertion (Matthew 19:3 and 1 Corinthians 7:15), but nowhere does Scripture *insist* on divorce, as if it's the only viable solution to a bad marriage. As I mentioned earlier, God hates it because he knows what happens when marriage is trivialized: whole families suffer and nations die.

Marvin Wilson, author of the marvelous book *Our Father Abraham: Hebrew Roots of the Christian Faith*, observes, "In this modern world it is relatively easy to get in and out of promises by saying such things as 'I've changed my mind,' or 'I just don't feel that way about you any more.' Words are often cheap. Among the Israelites, however, one's word was considered equal to one's promise."[4]

We say cynically, "Promises, promises." But the Hebrew word for "promise" implies *substance*. A Hebrew promise was a pledge of one's good faith to keep that promise by practical action—*until the promise was fulfilled.*

*Commitment is keeping your promises.* "When a man makes a vow to the Lord or takes an oath to obligate himself by a pledge, he must not break his word, but must do everything he said" (Numbers 30:2).

*"Many a man claims to have unfailing love, but a faithful man who can find?"* (Proverbs 20:6)

## KEEPING PROMISES IS GOD-LIKE

You know, David and Jill, keeping promises is not just about being the best, most honorable people we can be. Keeping promises is God-like. It's about our relationship with a faithful God. Without God, none of this makes sense. Without God, we have no point of reference for understanding faithfulness.

What can we know about God that will change the way we view marriage? "Know therefore that the Lord your God is God; he is the faithful God, keeping his covenant of love to a thousand generations of those who love him and keep his commands" (Deuteronomy 7:9).

And the prophet Jeremiah proclaimed, "Because of the Lord's great love we are not consumed, for his compassions never fail. They are new every morning; *great is your faithfulness*" (Lamentations 3:22-23).

So then, because God has created us in his image—and he is unwaveringly faithful—we must uphold faithfulness in the human community as the highest of virtues. You see, the big problem in America is that we've put God aside. We've taken him out of the government, out of the public schools, out of the media, out of the workplace. And now, worst of all imaginable things, we're taking him out of the family.

When you rip out your spiritual roots, the delicate planting of your lives will die. If Jesus is not at the center of your life and relationship, you will have no standard of faithfulness.

*The destruction of marriage in America is, at its core, rebellion against God.* We are not committed to one another anymore, because we don't love God anymore.

Without God, commitment is conditional.

With God, commitment is covenantal—a promise you can't break.

"The essence of marriage," writes Marvin Wilson, "the content, the bond, and the relationship which results—is covenant.... The rabbis regarded the Jewish marriage service as reflecting the main features of God's covenant with Israel at Mount Sinai. The covenant ceremony of marriage was seen as a reenactment of what happened at Sinai. It was designed to be a reminder of that basic covenant obligation which binds God to his people."[5]

## KEEPING YOUR WORD, EVEN IF IT KILLS YOU

In the Old Testament, "covenant" has two basic elements. First, it was eternal, as suggested by Hosea 2:19: "I will betroth you to me *forever*; I will betroth you in righteousness and justice, in love and compassion."

Second, it was sealed in blood. "Making a covenant" in Hebrew actually means "cutting a covenant." Animals were literally sliced in two, and the two persons cutting the covenant would walk side-by-side between the halves of the bloody carcass. The meaning was this: "May the very thing that has happened to this animal happen to me if I do not keep my promise."

Whoa! Dave and Jill, maybe we should have done something like that at your wedding. What do you think?

Actually, God did this once. In Genesis 15, God made a covenant with Abram (Abraham's earlier name). "Bring me a heifer," God said, "and a goat and a ram, each three years old."

Abram brought all these to him, cut them in two and arranged the halves opposite each other.... As the sun was setting, Abram fell into a deep sleep, and a thick and dreadful darkness came over him.... When the... darkness had fallen, a smoking firepot with a blazing torch appeared and passed between the pieces. On that day the Lord made a covenant [literally, "cut a covenant"] with Abram.

While Abram was in a trance, God, all by himself, passed between the halves of the carcasses. God was saying, in effect, "Let what happened to these animals happen to me, if this is what is necessary for me to keep my word."

Or, "I will do whatever I say. I guarantee it, *over my dead body....*"

Do you get it? God's encounter with Abram foreshadows the cross, where the Heavenly Father sealed his covenant with us in the blood of his own Son: "For God so loved the world that he gave his one and only son, that whoever believes in him shall not perish but have eternal life" (John 3:16).

Love is not just romantic feelings, or beautiful weddings. Love isn't the best imaginable sex. *Love is commitment. Love is faithfulness for a lifetime.*

"Our present age," wrote Marvin Wilson, "is one of shattered promises and broken relationships. An age sick with sentimentality has lost sight of the pledge 'till death do us part.' Love is often defined in all kinds of terms except commitment. We must return to Sinai [where God gave Moses the Ten Commandments], for there we are reminded through Hebrew eyes that marriage is just as serious and binding as that spectacular covenant ceremony on the day of revelation."[6]

The good news is that trends are taking us back to faithfulness in marriage. A recent article in *USA Today* announced, "Lawmakers counsel against divorce." The article reports, "The burgeoning movement to repeal no-fault divorce laws has spawned a campaign to encourage—or even compel—premarital counseling as a way to reduce America's sky-high divorce rate.

"Encouraged by church leaders, conservative politicians, and studies of the negative effects of divorce, lawmakers are looking at ways to promote happy marriages, or stop bad ones from ever getting started. About half of first-time marriages in the USA eventually fail—a statistic blamed for everything from high crime to school dropout rates."

That's the good news. The bad news is that no trend, or

politician, or law, will ever help the family. Ultimately, only spiritual renewal and obedience to God's laws will do that.

The fear of the Lord is the beginning of *wisdom—and faithfulness.*

After the conquest of Canaan, Joshua challenged the Israelites, "*Now fear the Lord and serve him with all faithfulness* [there's definitely a relationship between faithfulness and the fear of God].... But if serving the Lord seems undesirable to you [yes, God always gives us a choice; he even lets us choose to self-destruct], then choose for yourselves this day whom you will serve, whether the gods your forefathers served beyond the [Jordan] River, or the gods of the Amorites, in whose land you are living. *But as for me and my household, we will serve the Lord*" (Joshua 24:14-15).

Dave and Jill, can you say that together? Once a week?

"Let love and faithfulness never leave you; bind them around your neck, write them on the tablet of your heart. Then you will win favor and a good name in the sight of God and man" (Proverbs 3:3-4).

---

**LOOKING AHEAD: ... OUR CULTURE LOOKS FOR THE GREAT ESCAPE FROM ADVERSITY. WE'LL SACRIFICE ANYTHING TO THE GOD OF HAPPINESS. BUT ADVERSITY IS GOOD FOR YOU. DEAL WITH IT...**

---

## TWO

## NO SNIVELING

*Learning how to live through difficult times*

So what's your problem, Jill?

How big is your problem, Dave?

How big have you made your problem?

A fun article, "Whine of the times," appeared recently in *USA Today*. Subtitled, "Why is life so unfaaaair? The trivial can loom large among the self-obsessed," the article reported:

Whining is the anthem of the '90s.

Everyone knows the tune. It's the "Ehhhhhh" of all ages, the mew of the self-obsessed.

"Whining is a cross-generational malady. I'm gratified that once I turn 30, whining is something I can take with me," says 29-year-old Anthony Weiner (say "weener," not "whiner").

He's a city councilman in Brooklyn, "where we call it kvetching," and part of Generation X…

"We're all whiners," says Suzanne Rosenblum, 26, of Alexandria, Va., a museum curator. "We grew up watching baby-boomer TV shows in our formative years, when you were out and the baby-sitter was there."

But if baby boomers have taught the world to whine, the

X-ers have mastered the frequency of a fire drill siren.

Now we whine along with TV characters like Homer of "The Simpsons," "Seinfeld" sidekick George Costanza, Donna of "Beverly Hills 90210," and, of course, Hope and Michael, now showing in "thirty-something" reruns.

"Seinfeld is successful because he has found our whining threshold—22 minutes each week, broken up by commercials with people whining about what they're selling," Weiner says.

## SO WHAT ARE YOU WHINING ABOUT?

Your job?

The people you work with?

Your car?

Emission control and taxes in California?

Your sex life?

Your apartment?

Your in-laws?

Each other?

Dave and Jill, it's kind of hard for me to talk about this, because I feel like a hypocrite. Forget whining. You've both seen me go ballistic over nothin'. It's embarrassing, so when I bring up something that just happened to you, please try to listen to me anyway.

I'm thinking about your new car. You know, when it got "keyed" by one of your disgruntled employees. He was a real jerk, wasn't he? I was outraged, too. It's so difficult to be Christlike when people do rotten things to you.

But when the apostle Paul declared, "I have learned to be content *whatever* the circumstances" (Philippians 4:11), he wasn't just talking about "little" things, like getting your car vandalized. Paul had the best possible attitude in the worst case scenario. *Paul was in prison and he was full of joy!* He had either lost his mind, or he had discovered the real power of God's sustaining grace.

Dave, just think about your former youth pastor, Jeff. Now there's someone who has a real problem. As you know, his vivacious 32-year-old wife Kathy died of a devastating infection last month—just three weeks after giving birth to their fifth child.

What's he going to do?

I took Jeff to the Suns basketball game last week, just three weeks to the day after Kathy died. I'm sure he thought about that, but never mentioned it. We talked about how God's grace, along with the extraordinary support of our church family, is sustaining him one day at a time.

I'm writing this on Wednesday, the day I drag myself out of bed long before sunrise to lead our dreadfully early morning men's prayer meeting at the church.

It's something I've been doing every Wednesday for nearly seven years. You know me, Jill; how hard it is for me to get up early, unlike your mother-in-law, who wakes up with the chickens even though we live in the city.

Empathizing with my debility, someone at the church gave me a little plaque that reads: *If God wanted us to see the sunrise, he would have scheduled it later in the day.*

In our prayer meeting for a year or more, we've been creeping through the book of Acts a few verses at a time. Today, our Bible lesson was in Acts 16, the story of the apostle Paul and his friend, Silas, spending the night in a squalid dungeon. Human rights activists would have been appalled.

Well, as one of the men was sharing some of his personal ideas about the passage, God's light broke through my early morning mental fog with the thought: *there's not the slightest hint anywhere in this account that Paul and Silas felt victimized by people, circumstances, or God—even though they had every right to feel that way.*

Let me retell the story.

After helping to resolve an angry dispute in Jerusalem about whether Gentiles could become fully Christian without obeying all the laws of the Old Testament (they decided they could!), Paul and Silas headed out on what has been called Paul's Second Missionary Journey. There was just one little problem: they had already left Jerusalem, but they still weren't entirely sure where God was leading them (see Acts 16:6-8).

Kind of reminds me of young couples like you, who are sure they're in love, but they're equally unsure about what they're going to do with the rest of their lives. You need to be assured that, like Paul and Silas, God will guide you *along the way.*

I know this sounds radical, but the adventure is *not* in knowing exactly what God wants ahead of time so that you're sure never to make a mistake, but in discovering God's will together and learning one day at a time. Like Paul and Silas, you can't just sit there and wait for God to lead you in some spectacularly specific way. You gotta go somewhere! You gotta do something! (More on this in the chapter on "What to do?")

### HOW A DREAM BECOMES A NIGHTMARE

Well, Paul and Silas did just that, and one dark night, Paul had a vision of a man from Macedonia standing nearby and begging him, "Come over to Macedonia and help us" (16:9). You know, of course, that every night dream is not some mysterious clue about God's will for your life, but in Paul's case in Acts 16, it was like a personal phone call from God.

I'm sure Paul's ministry team was especially relieved. At last, Paul had a sense of God's leading! Enough of this trying-to-find-God's-will-in-the-process! On to Macedonia! No doubts now! God's word was clear!

Until they got there. Days went by without any fruitful ministry. No miracles. Nothin', until Paul cast a demon out of a psychic, sending the whole city into an uproar. Accusing them of starting a riot, the magistrates mercilessly flogged Paul and Silas and threw them into a miserable prison.

The Macedonian dream had become a Philippian nightmare. How could *this* be the will of God!

This is one of life's great questions: *if we made the right decision then, how could this be happening to us now?*

Or, if God really wanted us to get married, why are we having all these misunderstandings?

Or, if God really wanted us to move to California, why are we so lonely?

Or, if God really wanted us to live in this apartment, why are the neighbors so miserable?

The common assumption is that your decision in the first place was some terrible mistake, or that, somehow, you've been victimized by other people, or by your circumstances, or even by God himself.

So get mad. Talk about how unfair it is. Blame somebody for your problems. Blame God. Blame each other.

Let me repeat something I said earlier: *there's not the slightest hint in Acts 16 of Paul and Silas feeling victimized by people or circumstances or God, even though they had every right to feel that way.*

Whether or not Paul and Silas had lost their assurance of the will of God, we can only speculate. But one thing's for sure: they were confident that God was going to empower them to endure gracefully *whatever* happened to them.

### WHATEVER

Remember Bob Dole? The really old guy who ran against Bill Clinton in 1996? For a short while during the presidential campaign, the big news *du jour* was how the aging senator used "whatever" whenever—as a kind of filler word.

But "whatever" is one of the great words of the Bible! "I have learned to be content," Paul wrote in Philippians 4:12, "*whatever* the circumstances." He was in Rome at the time, not sightseeing or relaxing in the warm Italian sun, but in *another* prison. With iron chains draped from his raw wrists, Paul penned a love letter to his beloved Christian friends back in Philippi—the same city where he and Silas had been thrown into prison the very first time.

All things really do work together for good for those who love God and who are called according to his purposes (Romans 8:28). I love Eugene Peterson's masterful paraphrase of this verse: "That's why we can be so sure that every detail in our lives of love for God is worked into something good" (*The Message*).

Motivational speaker John Maxwell says it this way: "It's not what happens *to* you, it's what happens *in* you." In other words, you can't control your circumstances or the people in your life or each other, and you can't blame them either. *Whatever* happens, God will work in you his grace to make good come out of it. It's not whatever happens to you, it's what God does inside you, and he is far more concerned about your being content on the inside than happy on the outside.

## HOW BIG IS YOUR PROBLEM?
## HOW DO YOU DEAL WITH ADVERSITY?

Paul and Silas could not control what was happening to them in Philippi. Truth was, they had no one to blame but God because he had led them there. Their brutal imprisonment was an unanticipated outcome of doing the will of God, but these great men displayed no self-pity.

Some years ago, a poignant cartoon appeared in a thoughtful Christian magazine. The lead caption stated: "How Christians have coped through the ages." In the first of four frames, a New Testament Christian prays: "Lord, give me courage to face this accusing mob."

Things were really bad in the first century. It all began in Rome on that fateful day, July 19, A.D. 64, when Nero, the self-serving, lunatic emperor, torched his own city. Single-handedly, he turned Rome into a raging inferno.

Wooden buildings were jammed into one another in the streets of Rome. The avenues were narrow, and the flames spread like a desert grass fire on a hot, windy day. And then Nero blamed the Christians!

Imagine, if you will, the possibility of the church of Jesus Christ being blamed today for a severe economic downturn, or for riots in Los Angeles. Then visualize, David and Jill, our family—Mom and I, Shari and Matt—being arrested, having animal hides sewn to our bodies, being herded into a local football stadium, and having wild, half-starved animals turned loose on us.[1]

So how big is your problem? And how do you deal with adversity?

Back to the cartoon. In the second frame, the furrowed face of a Reformation Christian pleads, "Lord, help me declare your truth despite the cost." In the third, a young and frightened Eastern European couple, living in the dark terror of Stalinism, appeal to God: "Lord, may we persevere faithfully under these burdens."

In the final frame of the cartoon, a slick, 1990s American Christian burps out a little prayer to God: "Lord, the Audi's been running rough lately."

## LEARNING TO BE CONTENT

Paul—and countless other godly people throughout Christian history—learned how to be content *whatever* happened to them. A key word here is "learned." Contentment is not something that comes naturally. And the way you learn it has everything to do with your relationship with God. I'm convinced that people just can't make it without God.

Oh, yeah, they can get through a lot of things on their own. People pride themselves on being strong through tough times, but sooner or later they're going to feel utterly helpless. Like our friend, Jeff, a suddenly single dad with five kids.

How can it happen? How can people learn to be content *whatever*? With blatant simplicity, Paul answers the question: "I have *learned* to be content whatever the circumstances. I know what it is to be in need, and I know what it is to have plenty. I have *learned* the secret of being content in any and every situation, whether well fed or hungry, whether living in plenty or in want." What's Paul's secret? "I can do *everything* through himwho gives me strength" (Philippians 4:11-13).

Listen to the way this reads in *The Message*: "Actually, I don't have a sense of needing anything personally. I've learned by now to be quite content *whatever* my circumstances. I'm just as happy with little as with much, with much as with little. I've found the recipe for being happy whether full or hungry, hands full or hands empty. *Whatever* I have, wherever I am, I can make it through anything in the One who makes me who I am."

## NO SNIVELING

Paul *learned* how to be content by putting his trust in Jesus and allowing Jesus to do in him what he could not do in himself. I know this sounds really simplistic, but Paul just turned to the Lord.

He was doing it right then, in a Roman prison. He did it before, in the Philippian prison in Acts 16, the one we visited at the beginning of this chapter: "After they had been severely flogged, they were thrown into prison, and the jailer was commanded to guard them carefully. Upon receiving such orders, he put them in the inner cell and fastened their feet in stocks" (16:23-24).

And then it happened: *"About midnight, Paul and Silas were praying and singing hymns,* and the other prisoners were listening to them"* (16:25).

*Can you believe it?*

No poor victims here!

No whining.

No sniveling.

No self-pity.

Just Paul and Silas turning to the Lord.

And the Lord turning toward them: "Suddenly there was such a violent earthquake that the foundations of the prison were shaken. At once all the prison doors flew open, and everybody's chains came loose" (16:26).

Now I'm not sure you can conclude from this account that Paul's singing *caused* the earthquake, which *caused* the prison door to open. Sometimes prayer and praise may do that kind of thing, but God's plan in the Philippian prison was not just to post bail to release Paul from his personal misery, but to advance his kingdom purposes: to save the jailer and to give birth to a Christian community in Corinth.

I once had a woman tell me she wanted to divorce her husband and marry her husband's brother. She said that the Bible says God wants us happy. I told her I knew of no such verse and that our happiness is God's *last* concern. God wants me spiritually mature and content, and he knows that happiness can be contentment's greatest enemy. I know that, too. I raised you, Dave, and I often had the unclouded conviction that what made you fully happy was not going to make you a fully mature human being.

Happiness is when you are happy. Joy is when God has done so much in your life that you will bring happiness to others. But you don't just make them happy because you're fun to be around. Instead, you turn them on to God, just like Paul who brought joy to the Philippians in spite of his chains.

God is not limited by our chains, but we are limited by our faith.

## HOW TO BE HAPPY WHEN YOU HAVE
## EVERY REASON TO BE MAD

David and Jill, how did Paul do it? How did Paul keep such a great attitude? What were his secrets? There are clues all through Paul's correspondence with the Philippians.

*First, remind yourself that God is in control.* "In all my prayers for all of you, I always pray with joy," Paul wrote to the Philippians. "There has never been the slightest doubt in my mind that the God who started this great work in you would keep at it and bring it to a flourishing finish on the very day Christ Jesus appears" (1:3-6, *The Message*).

You've heard of life insurance?

Well, this is eternal life insurance, God's promise to make sure that his work in you gets done and gets done right. This gives me incredible confidence that God will work me through *whatever* whenever I'm stuck in the muck of the moment.

*Second, turn your obsession for yourself into love for others.* Aim your love energy away from yourself, like Paul: "And this is my prayer: that your love may abound more and more in knowledge and depth of insight, so that you may be able to discern what is best" (1:9-10).

"What is best" is what really matters.

When someone vandalizes your car, what really matters?

When a mother of five dies, what really matters?

Did I tell you about the vision? Just after Kathy's children had said their final good-byes to their mom, as they were leaving, two-year-old Adam, pointing to the outside window of his mommy's hospital room, blurted out two words: *"There's Jesus!"*

Paul and Silas were beaten senseless, but somehow they made it through. They survived because they could do anything through Christ who gave them strength. They were even able to praise God in the prison.

The death of a young mother of five is even more senseless, but Jeff is facing it through Christ who gives him supernatural strength. I've heard Jeff praise God, too.

How can you learn to be content *whatever?*

*Third, recognize the value in suffering and loss.* That's what Paul did: "Now I want you to know, brothers, that what has happened to me [that is, his imprisonment in Rome, just like his imprisonment in Philippi] has really served to advance the gospel. As a result, it has become clear throughout the whole palace guard and to everyone else that I am in chains for Christ" (1:12-13).

Keep reminding each other that *all* things work together for good. A forceful editorial in a recent issue of *Christianity Today* insisted that "the first task of the church in reinvigorating marriage is to reinvigorate peoples' consciousness of God, and to give meaning to sacrifice, forgiveness, suffering, disappointment, and, most important, love."[2]

## GETTING MARRIED TO BE MISERABLE

Did you get that? *One of the purposes of marriage is to give meaning to suffering and disappointment!*

*No, we don't get that.* We whine about our disappointments, and we're outraged by our suffering. We *expect* to be happy, that our job will make us happy, that our marriage will make us happy. It's not going to happen.

The truth is, we'll never find lasting happiness in those places. I heard a pastor tell this true story: At a church event he overheard the wife of a prominent leader in his church remark to a friend, "My husband doesn't make me happy."

That got his attention.

Listening in, he heard her continue: "I learned long ago that I would never be happy if I expected my husband to make me happy. I am happy when I choose to bring happiness into our marriage."

Classic Christian writer Thomas à Kempis understood this: "Whosoever knows best how to suffer will keep the greatest peace. That man is conqueror of himself, and lord of the world, the friend of Christ, and heir of Heaven."

And so did James. This is the Bible verse we all hate to hear: "When all kinds of trials and temptations crowd into your lives, my Christian friends, don't resent them as intruders, but welcome them as friends! Realize that they come to test your faith and to produce in you the quality of endurance. But let the process go on until that endurance is fully developed, and you will find you have become people of mature character, people of integrity with no weak spots" (James 1:2-4, J. B. Phillips).

David and Jill, you need to welcome adversity because you'll discover three things you'll never learn on your honeymoon:

- what you really need to know about yourself and God

- how helpless you are to control or even manage what's inside of you

- how to trust God in your helplessness to help you change.

One time I heard John Maxwell say, "People change when the pain of remaining the same becomes greater than the pain of changing." The value of suffering, then, is that it brings me to a point of reality and change, change that would *never* occur in me without the pain of suffering.

In case this is still not totally clear, let me batter you one more time with the same text in James from *The Message*: "Consider it a sheer gift, friends, when test and challenges come at you from all sides. You know that under pressure, your faith-life is forced into the open and shows its true colors. So don't try to get out of anything prematurely. Let it do its work so you become mature and well-developed, not deficient in any way."

How can you *learn* to be content *whatever*?

*Fourth, give up on what you want.* That's what Paul did: "For to me, to live is Christ and to die is gain" (1:21). A couple of chapters later he adds, "But whatever was to my profit I now consider loss for the sake of Christ. What is more, I consider everything a loss compared to the surpassing greatness of knowing Christ Jesus my Lord, for whose sake I have lost all things. I consider them rubbish that I may gain Christ" (Philippians 3:7-8).

What do you want?

What do you want from each other?

What's incredibly important to you?

What is it that you're not willing to give up that's more important than your love for Jesus? Or for each other?

*Really*, what's more important?

## HEAVEN ON EARTH

How can you *learn* to be content *whatever*?

*Fifth, always keep an eye on heaven:* "As long as I'm alive in this body," wrote Paul, "there is good work for me to do. If I had to choose right now, I hardly know which I'd choose. Hard choice! The desire to break camp here and be with Christ is powerful. Some days I can think of nothing better. But most days, because of what you are going through, I am sure that it's better for me to stick it out here. So I plan to be around for awhile" (1:22-25, *The Message*).

Older people are likely to tell you that life is short and that you need to make the most of every moment. Not too long ago I heard, on talk radio, an expert on terminal illness make an unnerving observation: "People die the way they live. If they live full of joy, they die full of joy. If they live full of malice and resentment, they die full of malice and resentment." Even if we can imagine that there is no hell, people bring their own hell with them when they die.

Or they bring heaven.

David and Jill, life is short, and heaven is your home, not your apartment. Thinking that way will give you perspective. "Most of us," Doug Murren writes, "are not overly endowed with perspective. Putting your life in perspective, whatever you suffer, is a great gift God can give you."

David and Jill, keep things in perspective, like Paul, who exclaimed, "So we're not giving up. How could we! Even though on the outside it often looks like things are falling apart on us, on the inside, where God is making new life, not a day goes by without his unfolding grace. These hard times are small potatoes compared to the coming good times, the lavish celebration prepared for us. There's far more here than meets the eye. The things we see now are here today, gone tomorrow. But the things we can't see now will last forever" (2 Corinthians 4:16-18, *The Message*).

It doesn't matter what happens *to* you, it matters what happens *in* you.

---

## AND NOW ... EVERYTHING YOU EVER WANTED TO KNOW ABOUT YOUR DAD'S SEX LIFE ...

---

THREE

## GOOD SEX

*Not everything you ever wanted to know,*
*but a few things you need to know*

Hey, are you looking around to see if anyone is watching you read this chapter?

Jill, did you turn to this chapter first?

Dave, are you curious about Mom and me?

Old people have sex, too.

When I was your age, I looked at people who were my age now and I wondered what it was like in their bedrooms. I mean, it wasn't a perverted kind of wondering, I just was curious if "it" happened a lot when you get older. And if "it" felt different.

You know what I discovered? It gets better.

Just a few weeks ago while channel surfing, I froze on the Letterman show. Tony Randall—I think he's about eighty— was talking smugly about his twenty-something pregnant wife, so young that her parents were about the right age to be Tony Randall's children. (I know, you have to stop and think about that one for a minute.)

I stared at Tony Randall's face and mumbled to myself, "How is that possible?" Even Letterman looked bewildered.

It's weird, thinking about old people having sex. Don't you agree?

However, no matter how old you are, the tough choices we

45

face about the gift of sex remain a fact of life. Our sexuality is not something we can take for granted. Ever. Sex is a powerful force that can bond a married couple into "one flesh"—or destroy them. I'm not talking just about sexual abuse or other kinds of sexual perversion you read about in the papers and see on daytime television. The gravest dangers are those in which temporal pleasures sear the conscience and scar the soul.

Last summer several of us from our church attended a conference in Baton Rouge, Louisiana. Looking for a nice place for an evening meal, we got lost in the south end of the city. On the right side of the road loomed a huge, gray unfinished high rise surrounded by a barbed-wire fence. Weeds were three and four feet high.

"What's *that*?" I blurted out.

A moment later someone pointed out a sign. It was the church, college, and international headquarters of the multi-million dollar Jimmy Swaggart ministries, now defunct and forsaken because of one man's secret sin. The once great man of God had preached with such passion about holiness, all the while shriveling inside from a sexual addiction.

## THE POISON OF MORAL FAILURE

Swaggart is not alone. Many people, often in visible positions in Christian circles, have been lured by various kinds of sexual temptation. Reputations are destroyed for life. Others, such as best-selling author Gordon MacDonald, whose first significant book was titled *Ordering Your Private World*, returned to the ministry only after years of healing and restoration. The temptation is real, and no one is immune.

It happened to a colleague and very personal friend, someone you both know, whose one night stand with a female counselee nearly destroyed his family and ministry. Again, God's grace and healing have prevailed.

A pastor friend told me about a man in his church who was arrested for soliciting sex. A *leader* in the church, he had been buying sex for *twenty years* and no one had a clue, not even his wife.

Recently *Leadership Magazine* commissioned a poll of a thousand pastors. The pastors indicated that 12 percent of them had committed adultery while in the ministry. That's one out of eight! And 23 percent had done something they considered sexually inappropriate.

*Christianity Today* surveyed a thousand of its subscribers who were *not* pastors and found the figure to be nearly double: one in four Christian men are unfaithful and nearly one half admitted behaving themselves improperly![1]

Sex. It's the best of times and the worst of times. It's awesome when it's right, and unspeakably destructive when it's wrong. In fact, sexual irresponsibility may be, more than anything else, the razor knife shredding the fabric of our nation. And I predict, without knowing a thing about your personal life, David and Jill, that sexual misunderstanding will be one of two or three of the most serious issues you will face as a couple.

I have lots of reasons for believing this, my own struggles in this area notwithstanding. But before I talk about me, let me help you understand what you're up against: *We have a cultural obsession with sex, which entices us to the precipice of unrealistic expectations, where we risk tumbling into a personal hell of sexual fantasies, sexual addiction, and spiritual oppression.*

## THE INSATIABLE SEARCH FOR GOOD SEX

An article in the women's section of the Phoenix newspaper blared: "Writing the book on good sex." The report admitted in its opening statement: "The American culture's *insatiable search for good sex*—especially good sex for women [Does this imply that good sex for men is not as hard to find?] apparently has no limit.

"We've had Masters and Johnson, the Kinsey Report, the Hite Report, the new Kinsey Report, *The Joy of Sex*, the G spot and now CAT, not to mention the *Kamasutra* and the mythical 'Venus butterfly.' Here are four books [which the article reviews] that indicate that the search is still in full swing."[2]

If you really don't think Americans—both men and women—are in a frenzy about sex, just scan the covers of the most popular magazines. Columnist James J. Kilpatrick noted in a recent editorial that "apart from *Science, National Geographic* and *Southern Living*, it is hard to find a popular magazine that doesn't revel in sex. *Cosmopolitan* positively wallows in sex. Even *Reader's Digest*, eager for a piece of the action, regularly instructs in the sexual side of marriage."

Who are our role models? Madonna? Dennis Rodman in drag? Alternative rock bands and rappers, whose tunes vomit vulgarity, violence, and sexual perversion?

What about motion pictures? Or television with "adult themes?" Did you know that TV standards at the time demanded Beaver Cleaver's parents sleep in *twin* beds? That was just forty years ago. Back then, today's guidelines for general viewing would be considered pornographic.

Morton Kondracke, a senior editor of *The New Republic* and a certified liberal, startled his "progressive" readers by admitting, "We prudes [he's including himself!] just think that sexual liberation has gone way too far, that all kinds of people are suffering as a result, and that the media, the churches, schools, the government, and other influential grown-ups ought to encourage old-fashioned virtues—like self-discipline and the postponement of gratification—instead of encouraging young people to screw their brains out."[3]

## A LINGERIE SHOW ON SUNDAY MORNING

David and Jill, you know my pastor friend, Mark Buckley? A very funny guy! Well, a couple of months ago he was holding up the newspaper as he read an article to his congregation. It wasn't a humorous piece, but people were snickering.

Unnerved, he interrupted his sermon: "What's so funny?"

Seeing them pointing to the *back side* of the newspaper, Mark flipped it over. To his embarrassment, there on the other side, was a full page and particularly-risque lingerie advertisement.

It's everywhere!

I know you're going to scream at this one: I think that the emergence of popular lingerie stores like Victoria's Secret, a refined, upscale sex shop, is symptomatic of our quest for the ultimate sexual experience.

Yeah, I admit it, Mom and I have shopped there, too. I've even ordered her stuff from their catalog, and I don't think that's blatantly sinful. But Victoria's Secret is a tiny symptom of a huge problem: *the totally unrealistic expectations of our cultural obsession with sex.* Pleasure becomes the purpose of sex, and sex becomes an end in itself.

We gawk at the sex scenes at Harkins and AMC, and we buy pleasure at Victoria's Secret. Problem is, our bedrooms seem so sterile compared with what we imagine it should be like. Our lovemaking is never quite what we think it could be, or it's not what it could be frequently enough.

So our disappointment with one another begins to grow, little by little, gnawing away at us inside. Maybe we just don't love each other anymore. No pleasure in sex *must* mean there's no love in our hearts. You know, we've lost that lovin' feelin'.

## SEX IS SPIRITUAL

And that's the whole problem: sex isn't just a loving feeling. It's not just for pleasure. It's *spiritual.* Let me explain.

On the down side, sex is like a god, because whatever controls your life is your god, like it or not, admit it or not. The truth, though, is that sex is *from* God. Sex is spiritual because it was God's idea:

Then the Lord God made a woman from the rib he had taken out of the man, and he brought her to the man.
The man said,
   "This is now bone of my bones
   and flesh of my flesh;

she shall be called 'woman,'
  for she was taken out of man."
For this reason a man will leave his father and mother and be
united to his wife, and they will become one flesh. The man
and his wife were both naked, and they felt no shame.

GENESIS 2:22-25


God made sex on purpose for four reasons *in the following
order*.

1. spiritual union—"one flesh"

2. companionship and intimacy—"naked and not ashamed"

3. having children—"Adam lay with his wife Eve, and she
   became pregnant" (Genesis 4:1-2).

4. for pleasure—which isn't mentioned at all in Genesis, but for
   fun look up Proverbs 5:18-19.

Sex is spiritual, because our sexuality is God-given for God's
sake. I know this may sound silly, but this is why couples feel "so
close" sitting in church together. Just today, one of the younger
guys on our church staff remarked about how he enjoys sitting
close to his wife in church. "I like my hand on her leg," he said
with a sly smile.

I know in our case, the few times we sit together in church as
a family (I'm usually preaching), Mom *loves* it if I hold her hand
or put my arm around her. *Spiritual intimacy leads to personal
intimacy, which leads to sexual intimacy.* It *never* works the other
way around. Good sex has nothing to do with technique and
everything to do with intimacy. It's the way God made us.

*Godly sex is a beautiful thing!* Does that sound weird?
Somebody even did some research on this. A few years ago
Focus on the Family published a report about sexual satisfaction.
They found, contrary to popular opinion, that the more conser-

vative (godly? prudish?) a person's view of sex, the greater the likelihood of sexual satisfaction, while the more "liberated" a person's views on sex, the less the likelihood of sexual satisfaction.[4]

Ever hear the Stones' Mick Jagger? He crooned the pain of my generation: "I can't get no ... saaaa ... tisfaction." Let me say it again: pursue pleasure with passion and you'll end up with emptiness and pain. Pursue God with passion, and you'll have pleasure in the bedroom.

The world has it backwards, so "God gave them over in the sinful desires of their hearts to sexual impurity for the degrading of their bodies with one another. They exchanged the truth of God for a lie, and worshiped and served created things rather than the Creator" (Romans 1:24-25).

Leave God out of your sex life and you end up in a vacuum of unfulfilled pleasure. So what do people do to fill the vacuum? When you serve the god of lust, you'll do anything. Let me repeat: *We have a cultural obsession with sex, which entices us to the precipice of unrealistic expectations, where we risk tumbling into a personal hell of sexual fantasies, sexual addiction, and spiritual oppression.*

And pornography.

## AN AFFAIR OF THE MIND

Last week, Larry Greenwald, director of counseling at our church, handed me a new book by Laurie Hall, *An Affair of the Mind: One Woman's Courageous Battle to Salvage Her Family from the Devastation of Pornography.* Like so many other books people hand me to read, I stuck it away in my personal library next to the other books about sex. "Good resource," I told myself.

But just a week later, Gwen Ellis, my editor at Servant

Publications, happened to mention this same book—and that I should read it. It would help me, she thought, get a feel for how I should write this book.

Man, is it powerful! Included in *An Affair of the Mind* is a collection of letters Laurie Hall wrote to her wayward husband, Jack. Here's a sample:

> Dear Jack,
>
> I meant every word I said to you that day twenty years ago, all that stuff about loving, honoring, cherishing, and forsaking all others. Did you mean it, too, or did you just mouth the words? How could you mean them when from day one for you this marriage has been about lust, not love?
>
> Ironic isn't it, how lust destroys the very thing it lusts after until, at the end, the thing being consumed has no beauty that anyone would desire? Lust never has enough. When the magazines weren't enough, you went to the strip shows; and when they weren't enough, you bought the girls and took them back to your hotel room. And it didn't matter how many of them you had, it was never enough.
>
> Now I've had enough. Enough hurting. Enough crying. Enough hoping.[5]

Just typing out the letter for this chapter makes *me* feel like crying.

Now David and Jill, you are such a fine Christian couple, and I could *never* imagine this happening to you. But it happens to fine Christian couples, and but for the grace of God, it could happen to me.

I have plenty in my life for God to forgive, but honestly, I have never in my adult life looked at pornographic literature. I did, though, when I was a kid. Yeah, just a kid. I used to babysit for a family down the street when I was thirteen or fourteen, and they had copies of *Playboy* in the magazine rack in the front room.

I looked and wham! It wasn't just the pictures, it's what they did to me, how they aroused me. That was the first and *only* time in my life I *experienced* pornography, and those images still haunt me.

The temptation, though, never goes away. Not even when you are almost fifty. There it is, that filthy stuff, peeking out at you from behind the counter of every convenience market. Right there, next to all the good magazines on every newsstand at every airport.

Hey, who's gonna notice? I'm alone. Just one little look won't hurt.

And more! Skin flicks readily available at video rental stores, "adult" channels on cable, and the latest lust—pornography on the Internet.

To ease you in slowly, check out all the sort-of-pornography in R-rated movies and wildly suggestive photography in popular magazines like *People* and *Us*—and the Victoria's Secret catalog.

## LYING, DEAD, OR GAY

Any guy who says he isn't tempted sexually is lying, dead, or gay. Men are just plain unrealistic about their sexual vulnerability and the profound consequences of not controlling themselves.

A couple of years ago a friend told me a story about his brother, who was in a second marriage. His wife had a teenage daughter still living at home. In the middle of the night, in a crazed moment of sexual fantasy, he went into his sleeping step-daughter's room and touched her in the wrong place. She awoke screaming, and the man's life was nearly ruined.

In the end, he became a Christian through the ensuing trauma, and miraculously, God healed the marriage. But what would come over a man to do something like that? And risk everything?

I think women are not always realistic about male sexuality either. Most women think their husbands are oversexed (not true) and that they think about sex a lot (probably true). And *Christian* husbands are supposed to be different in their sexual needs (not true).

Yeah, I know that women like to look at buff guys, but the fact is that 90 percent or more of pornographic literature targets lust in men. And if you didn't know this, Jill (and all the other women reading this book), you should: it's common for men to use pornography to masturbate.

Are you shocked?

Pornography arouses a man's lust, but according to Dr. Victor Cline, a prominent researcher on the psychological effects of pornography, it also contains scientifically inaccurate, false, and misleading information about human sexuality, especially female sexuality. The man who reads it, then, brings distortions and dysfunctions into his own sexual identity.[6]

So when a woman hands her man a pornographic magazine to help him along in his sexual arousal (I've heard this is not uncommon), it will do just the opposite of what she thinks. Pornography dehumanizes both the woman in the picture and the man who looks at her.

But even worse than that, yes, even worse, *pornographic magazines and movies drive people into a personal hell of sexual addiction and spiritual oppression.*

## SEX AND THE DEVIL

Remember? Sex is spiritual, *powerfully* spiritual. When you start with relationship with God, you get unconditional intimacy ("one flesh"—Genesis 2:24) and sex without shame ("both naked, and they felt no shame"—Genesis 2:25). Start with pleasure and leave God out (pornography) and you toy with sexual addiction, maybe even spiritual oppression.

Laurie Hall, in a short section in *An Affair of the Heart* called "Things That Go Bump in the Night," reports the following anonymous story:

> Early one morning, four-year-old Tommy walked into his parents' bedroom.
>
> "Who's that man?" he asked, pulling on his mother to wake her up.
>
> "What man?" Sue said, blinking herself awake.
>
> "That man all dressed in black next to Daddy," he said.
>
> She could see no one next to Matt. "Tommy, there is no one standing next to Daddy. You go back to bed."
>
> "Yes there is, Mommy," and Tommy began to cry.
>
> Over the next few weeks, Tommy saw the man several times. Sue dismissed each incident as the overactive imagination of a four-year-old. Then, one night, she was awakened by Matt reaching for her.
>
> "Sue," he croaked, "pray for me."
>
> She could see terror written across Matt's face. Quickly, she stammered out a prayer, asking God to come and be with them and take care of whatever was scaring her husband.
>
> Later, Matt told her that he had awakened to see the form of a man hovering over him. "It was like a heaviness. I could hardly breath, Sue," he said.
>
> Although Sue was unaware of it at that time, Matt had been struggling with a secret sexual addiction that involved masturbation and exhibitionism."[7]

The point of this account is that our sexuality is spiritual, and sex just for pleasure runs the real risk of spiritual oppression and control. Now I'm not suggesting that every sexual sin is demonic, but spiritual warfare is real, and our lives interface with the spiritual dimension. That's why Peter writes, "Keep a cool head. Stay alert. The Devil is poised to pounce, and would like nothing better than to catch you napping. Keep your guard up" (1 Peter 5:8-9, *The Message*).

I know, some of this is really gross stuff, but the truth must be told—to you and your generation. Knowledge of all this garbage will help you understand the power of sex, for both good and evil, and how terribly important it is for you to keep your sex life in line with God's Word.

## THE BIBLE ON SEX

Listen to this extraordinary translation of 1 Corinthians 6:16-20 by Eugene Peterson: "There's more to sex than mere skin on skin. Sex is as much spiritual mystery as physical fact. As written in Scripture, 'The two become one.' Since we want to become spiritually one with the Master, we must not pursue the kind of sex that avoids commitment and intimacy, leaving us more lonely than ever—the kind of sex that can never 'become one.'

"There is a sense in which sexual sins are different from all others. In sexual sin we violate the sacredness of our own bodies, these bodies that were made for God-given and God-modeled love, for 'becoming one' with another. Or didn't you realize that your body is a sacred place, the place of the Holy Spirit? Don't you see that you can't live however you please, squandering what God paid such a high price for?

"The physical part of you is not some piece of property belonging to the spiritual part of you. God owns the whole works. So let people see God in and through your body" (*The Message*).

## BRUTAL HONESTY IS THE BEST POLICY

It's important, Jill, for you to have the freedom to ask David at anytime what he's thinking. Or if he's been looking at things he shouldn't. He probably won't volunteer the information on his own if he is, because there's shame in lust.

In some ways, it's what every guy dreads—a woman who wants his heart. A man wants inside a woman, *physically*. A woman wants inside a man, *spiritually and emotionally*. Even some of the most liberal experts on human sexuality agree that a man's *primary* pleasure in sex is physical, while a woman's is relational. Now there are exceptions. Both men and women want both physical pleasure and emotional bonding, but generally women are more sensitive to relational issues.

In a secular book titled *Why Can't Men Open Up?*, Steven Naifeh and Gregory Smith explore men's fear of intimacy: "Why can't men open up? That question, bursting with frustration and exasperation, was first thrown at us during a women's discussion-group meeting we attended as part of the research for a book on sexual relationships. Expecting to catch some choice inside tips on how women like to have men make love, we found instead that making love was not really on their minds.

"Jennifer, who hosted the meeting, told us, 'Speaking for myself, when things are going well in my relationship with my husband, the sex is good. When they're not, the sex is awful. It's as simple as that.'"[8]

Remember, I said earlier I would come back to talking about intimacy? Well, here we are! *Sexual* intimacy is rooted in *relational* intimacy. Dr. Miriam Stoppard, medical doctor and author of twenty-seven health books, has a message for the nineties: "The best sex occurs in long-term, stable relationships.

"It's simply unrealistic to expect satisfying sex with a large number of people during short sexual encounters. It takes years of getting to know each other, getting to understand each other, learning what turns each other on.

"We have been so preoccupied with the physical side of sex that we've forgotten the joys of what was known as 'marital' sex—which is all about giving love and oneself totally to another person over a long period of time."[9]

How do you achieve relational intimacy? It will require daily effort for the rest of your life! *Before* sin, Adam and Eve were naked and they had no shame. *Nothing* interfered with their intimacy. *After* sin, though, they became self-conscious and self-protective. They sewed fig leaves together, the Bible says, to cover their butts. (Well, it doesn't say it *exactly* that way, but you know what the expression means.)

Anyway, fig leaves are about hiding—hiding your shame from others. Hiding from yourself. Hiding from God. Practically, Adam and Eve's fig leaves meant they couldn't really talk to one another honestly anymore, because they had something to hide.

## LIAR, LIAR

Listen to how Adam responded when God found him cowering in the Garden of Eden: "The woman [it's her fault] you put her with me [it's God's fault]—she gave me some fruit from the tree, and I ate it [I just couldn't help myself] (Genesis 3:12)."

Eve was no less devious: "The serpent," she said, "deceived me, and I ate (Genesis 3:13)." The devil made her do it.

It's the language of a liar, someone who has something to hide. It's the dishonest communication of self-deception and denial. When you're listening to someone like that, you don't know what to believe. You don't know whom to believe. You're so confused.

But God has a solution for the fig leaves and for what they

represent. It's the skin of animals, a prophetic symbol of Jesus shedding his blood and dying for you and me, in order to cover our sins, to forgive us and clothe us with his righteousness.

To *put on* the skin of animals, though, Adam and Eve had to *take off* the fig leaves of their denial and face once again their own nakedness and shame. This is huge. This is why it's so terribly difficult to get healed. It feels like we have so much to lose.

Imagine, taking off all those fig leaves right there in front of each another. It's easier to take off your clothes. But taking off your clothes will become less and less rewarding if you don't take off the fig leaves. Open up. Get honest with each other. You won't have sex every day, but you must work on your intimacy every day, and you need Jesus to help you. So when you have sex, you'll howl, "This is good! This is *really* good!"

Let me suggest some tips for building relational intimacy:

- Be honest with each other. A half truth is a whole lie. Now I don't mean, "Lay it on the table! Get everything off your chest." Sometimes, when people say, "I'm going to be really honest with you," what they mean is, "I'm really angry and I'm gonna be real nasty."

  Sometimes, though, the timing is everything. Some things need to be talked about at just the right time. The end of the day is probably not the best time.

- Talk about lots of things, so when you need to talk about important things, talking will come more easily. And remember that communication is not just language. Words, some communications experts tells us, are only about 10 percent of the message. Voice tone is 40 percent, and non-verbal communication—body language, facial expression—is as much as 50 percent of what we "say"!

- Listen up, guys. Not just to the words, but to the feelings behind the words. Men don't like to admit this, but people—

women *and men*—are basically emotional about *everything*. Don't believe me? Pay careful attention to television advertising. Stand back and watch how they get to your heart, to your feelings. So communication is not just about what we say, but about what we are feeling when we speak.

Human relations guru Steven Covey in his best-selling book *Seven Habits of Highly Effective People*, wrote, "When another person speaks, we're usually 'listening' at one of four levels. We may be *ignoring* another person, not really listening at all.

"We may practice *pretending*. 'Yeah. Uh-huh. Right.'

"We may practice *selective listening*, hearing only certain parts of the conversation. We often do this when we're listening to the constant chatter of a preschool child.

"Or we may even practice *attentive listening*, paying attention and focusing energy on the words that are being said. But very few of us ever practice the fourth level, the highest form of listening, *empathetic listening*."[10]

You can practice listening by giving feedback, not just on the fact you hear, but on what you think the other person is feeling, like "What I heard you say is..." Or, "What I think you're feeling is..."

Solomon said, "He who answers before listening—that is his folly and his shame" (Proverbs 18:13).

Think about this. There are four barriers to empathetic listening:

1. evaluating;
2. probing—digging around and forcing the conversation to go your way;
3. advising;
4. interpreting.

• Pray together. Pray for each other. Pray alone. Because prayer is intimacy with God, it enhances your intimacy with one another. This is one of the reasons, I'm convinced, why men struggle to pray out loud with their wives, because it makes them feel like they are undressing emotionally. It makes them feel vulnerable. Naked in the wrong way.

Dr. Bernie Zibergeld comments, "One of the cornerstones of the masculine stereotype in our society is that a man is one who has no doubts, questions, or confusion about sex, and that a real man knows how to have good sex and does so frequently. For a man to ask a question about sex, thereby revealing ignorance, or to express concern, or to admit to a problem is to risk being thought something less than a man."[11]

- No one's perfect when it comes to relational intimacy and sex, so the worst thing you can do is hide behind your ignorance and never reach out and get help. If you need it, *get help!* There are lots of good books and many good and godly people out there who are just waiting to help you.

- You need accountability with other people—David with other guys and Jill with other women.

- Don't allow yourself to be in situations that compromise your moral convictions. Like Doug Murren said about perspective, understand that little moral compromise now can destroy your life later.

---

### LOOKING AHEAD... HOW TO GET DAVID TO

### WASH THE DISHES...

---

## FOUR

## WHY CAN'T WE ALL
## JUST GET ALONG?

*Gender stereotypes, marriage myths,
and irreconcilable differences*

"Racism is endemic."

Warren Stewart, Pastor of the First Institutional Baptist Church in urban Phoenix and perhaps the most influential African American in our state, said this to me over a steaming plate of enchiladas in downtown Phoenix.

I initiated the luncheon because I wanted to get to know this man, the spokesperson for the hard-fought Martin Luther King state holiday here in Arizona. A deeply spiritual person, he has also participated in predominantly white pro-life demonstrations, which, he pointed out to me, is unusual for a leader in the black community.

For him, civil rights and the rights of the unborn are mutually inclusive concerns. Essentially, both are part of the same problem.

It's endemic ... the problem, that is.

"What's that word mean?" you ask. (If it's any consolation to your ignorance, I never really thought about the word either until I had lunch with Warren Stewart.)

When Pastor Stewart stated, without a hint of bitterness, "Racism is endemic," he meant that it's deeply embedded in the human condition. It's right there in *everybody's* heart. Ever hear a racial slur? Or a joke about Polish people? Mexicans? Jews?

Let me tell you something else that's right there in every-body's heart: sexism. Ever hear a joke about dumb blondes? Or women drivers? I have a book of dumb men jokes. Some of them are really funny, but others make no sense to me. I wonder if they make sense to women?

Just as there are racial stereotypes bursting with misunder-standing, pain, and hostility, there are myths about gender and marriage. The assumption that people with a particular skin color are always like this and never like that, or that men and women should or should not do certain things, or should act or not act in certain ways, is a symptom of soul disease, a malevo-lent melanoma of the human heart.

God, you see, created men and women different on pur-pose—*he created people different*—to live in interdependent part-nership. Every snowflake is unique, every fingerprint unlike any other. The wondrous beauty of God's creation is in the aggre-gate harmony of infinite difference. That's heaven!

*But there's no heaven on earth because there's hell in our hearts.*

It's why there's so much denial and why we all feel like vic-tims. It's why our relationships are so shallow and difficult, and why people do such dastardly things to one another.

*It's why so many marriages end in divorce.*

### UNPLUGGED

You've probably heard of Alvin Toffler. More than twenty-five years ago, he wrote his classic book, *Future Shock*, about what our world is coming to. It was a book about trends that started a trend of books about trends.

Toffler is the guy who first called us a "throw-away" genera-tion, and he wasn't just talking about how Styrofoam packaging could bring about an ecological crisis. Uncovering a covert effect of urbanization, Toffler wrote about how we throw away people like used appliances. He even coined a term for it: "modular relationships," where, like a power cord on a hair dryer, we just plug into and unplug from people for strictly pragmatic reasons.

A personal experience with an electronics salesperson at Montgomery Ward comes to mind. I bought a stereo system there a few years ago, and because it was a floor sample, I had some difficulty getting all the paperwork. The salesman assured me he would take care of it, but a week or two went by and I heard nothing.

So I called and left a message.

Still nothing.

After several more unsuccessful attempts to reach him, I got aggravated. (Can you imagine that, Dave and Jill? Me getting aggravated?) Asking for a supervisor, I gave him an earful. You know, sometimes we represent these little outrages like they're the worst thing that ever happened to us.

"So what are you going to do about it?" I demanded.

"I'll take care of it immediately for you, sir. I'm also sorry our employee did not return your calls. He's been out of town. His mother is dying."

*Selah.**

"Thank you," I said with a suddenly mellow voice. "And I'm terribly sorry to hear that."

I swallowed hard as I hung up the phone. I had felt anger toward the man who broke his promise to help me (so I thought), but the possibility of his facing a personal trauma never entered my modular mind. All I cared about was prompt

---

*Selah, an Old Testament word used periodically in the Psalms, means "stop and think about that for awhile."

and courteous service. You see, he was *just* a salesperson. Beyond that, he had no other value as a human being. It was a *modular relationship*, as opposed to "total relationship," another Toffler term.

What we don't realize is that this modular relationship mentality affects *all* our relationships, including our most important ones: spouse, family, and best friends.

## TRADING IN OLD, USED RELATIONSHIPS

Years ago I traded in our old black van, the one we took to the East Coast on a family vacation when you kids were small. We still have wondrous memories of that trip: Niagara Falls, Gettysburg, and Washington D. C.; and you, David, and your little sister, Shari, smacking each other with your giant swirly souvenir suckers. Remember? Your sucker shattered and hers didn't.

Clearing the old van of a few last personal things, I paused there in the back lot of the auto dealership to take a last, wistful look at our family vehicle. And then, with a rush of excitement, I slipped behind the wheel of my new car and drove away.

I know, it sounds cheesy. But I'm making a point. The thought occurred to me at the time: This is sort of how people feel about relationships. About divorce. About second and third marriages. We drown our pain in a false sense of freedom—or in the rush of a brand-new relationship.

Now I'm not insensitive to what divorce does to people. It's certainly not as simple as trading in an old car. It's more like wrecking your new Mustang convertible and ending up in an intensive care unit. It's horrible. Yet there are uncanny similarities, because it's become so easy to unplug from our connections with others, even our *closest* relationships. I've been there, I've had it happen to me. I've been betrayed.

Easy-in, easy-out relationship is a cultural cancer. Everybody has it, and it's killin' us, but nobody knows we have it. It's why police-beating victim Rodney King, during the Los Angeles riots, on national television, with the night sky flaming fire-orange behind him, moaned incredulously,

*"Why can't we all just get along?!"*

## WELL, WHY CAN'T WE ALL JUST GET ALONG?

Let me suggest a simple answer: *sin.*

*Sin is endemic.*

Psychologists and sociologists may object to this old-fashioned idea that people are basically sinful, but no one disputes our national decline, or that we are adrift in a sea of moral decay, or that human beings are profoundly self-centered and dysfunctional.

Hey! Maybe I'm a simpleton, but to me "sin" is just the biblical and theological term for the mess we're in. Just a few weeks ago, a timely editorial appeared in the *Arizona Republic* about how America has become a cult of individualism. The article was revisiting a theme I had seen a couple of years ago in an article where a sociologist, Robert Bellah, said he felt a heritage of individualism had brought Americans to the point of thinking that there is no such thing as the common good except as the sum of individual goods.

Bellah went on to say that because we live in such a complex, interdependent world, the sum of our individual goods produces a common bad that eventually erodes our individual satisfactions.

Bellah, of the University of California at Berkeley [not known for its Bible-waving professors] and author of the 1985 best seller *Habits of the Heart*, told a meeting of Episcopal bishops that such individualism tends to make religion radically subjective and private.

You know what people say: "We live in a free country." What they really mean is: "I can do whatever I please." The attitude's ancient: "In those days Israel had no king, so the people did whatever seemed right in their own eyes" (Judges 21:25, *New Living Translation*).

So the rights of the criminal become more important than the rights of the victim. More important, it seems, than social order. And the rights of the student become more important than order in the public schools. And the rights of the individual become more important than marriage and the family.

It's a free country.

## GOTTA DO WHAT'S BEST FOR ME

Dave and Jill, you've probably heard people say, "I gotta do what's best for me." Usually, they're talking about ending some relationship. Well, the fact is that what's best for you may not always be the best for all the other people in your life.

What was best for Jesus—staying in heaven—was definitely not what was best for the rest of us. But he did the best thing. He put his own personal feelings aside and willingly suffered a vicious death—for you and me: "This is how we've come to understand and experience love: Christ sacrificed his life for us. This is why we ought to live sacrificially for our fellow believers, and not just be out for ourselves" (1 John 3:16, *The Message*).

That's why, Paul appeals, "If you've gotten anything at all out of following Christ, if his love has made any difference in your life, if being in a community of the Spirit means anything to you, if you have a heart, if you *care*—then do me a favor: Agree with each other, love each other, be deep-spirited friends.

"Don't push your way to the front; don't sweet-talk your way to the top. Put yourself aside, and help others get ahead. Don't be obsessed with getting your own advantage. Forget yourselves long enough to lend a helping hand" (Philippians 2:1-5, *The Message*).

It's the gospel. It's a message as old as Christianity. Jesus had to intervene because our self-centeredness and sin stand in the way of unconditional relationships. Jesus came to bear the penalty of our sins, to destroy sin's power over us, and to empower us to interface with others in the way God planned it from the beginning.

## IS GOD MALE OR FEMALE?

Sin is endemic.

Sin is the root of racism.

Sin is the root of genderism.

Sin is the reason why we all can't just get along because it's the perversion of relationship as God originally intended it in Genesis 1:27:

> So God created man in his own image,
> in the image of God he created him,
> male and female he created them.

This little poem-like statement is what Bible scholars call "Hebrew parallelism," which links the ideas of each of the parallel statements. Here in Genesis 1:27 it means that the image of God is male and female. *Both!*

In other words, it takes both man and woman—all of us together—to fully represent and experience God. It was *never* God's intent to create a cult of individuals—little dribbles of humanity, isolated in their private lives by private interests, divided by gender and racial hostilities.

The world is a system, ecologically and socially, like an orchestra, where all the littlest parts are supposed to harmonize in a cosmic symphony. Everything was made to fit, but the curse of sin is like dumping a hundred different jigsaw puzzles together—and thoroughly mixing them.

Well, why can't we just put it together?

Well, why can't we just get along?

Well, we can't ... without Jesus. When you are in the middle of a maddening puzzle of irreconcilable problems, your only option is to turn to Jesus: "For he himself is our peace, who has made the two one, and has destroyed the barrier, *the dividing wall of hostility*[1] ... through the cross, by which he put to death their hostility" (Ephesians 2:14-16).

Difference is divine, Godlike. It comes right from God. To value difference is to honor God. But because sin is endemic, we turn our differences into war zones.

Sin-driven hostility is what you feel about the unhelpful salesperson at Montgomery Ward. It's what you feel about the guy on the freeway who's driving too slow. It's what you think when you see skin that's a different color. It's the bad things, Dave and Jill, that you will feel about each other more often than you would probably like. It's why we can't all get along.

## HOW WE CAN ALL GET ALONG

Jesus put to death our hostility *through the cross*, bringing the real possibility of peace on earth and goodwill to all people. Jesus is the *Prince* of Peace, and the cross is why we can all get along: "Therefore, if anyone is in Christ, he is a new creation; the old has gone, the new has come! All this is from God, who reconciled us to himself through Christ, and gave us the ministry of reconciliation: that God was reconciling the world to himself in Christ, *not counting men's sins against them*" (2 Corinthians 5:17-19).

The message of reconciliation is that God doesn't count our sins against us. Guess what, that's the only way, David and Jill, that you can be reconciled to each other, by not counting your sins against each other.

*Jesus in me empowers me to value difference and forgive your sins against me.* I know, sometimes that seems *impossible*. Well, think about it. The healing of our broken relationship with God, because of our sin, is *impossible* without the intermediary work of the cross. Christians believe this is the most important teaching of the New Testament!

What's not so popularly understood is that the cross was intended to work two ways: vertically, to heal our irreconcilable differences with God, and horizontally, to heal our irreconcilable differences with each other. The cross *must* stand between us and the Heavenly Father, but the cross also *must* stand between you and me.

Oh, yeah, I can get along with anybody, as long as they get along with me. But when they push the relationship to the point of popping, only the extreme love of Christ, only the work of the cross in my heart, will penetrate the gloom of insult and pain. Not only do I need the cross and God's unconditional forgiveness *for* me, I need the work of the cross and God's unconditional forgiveness *in* me: "Get rid of all bitterness, rage and anger, brawling and slander, along with every form of malice." *Every form of malice?* Whoa! "Be kind and compassionate to one another, forgiving each other, just as in Christ God forgave you" (Ephesians 4:31-32).

God created us to be *interdependent*, like the rest of his created order. Sin makes us ferociously *independent*, like the guy who torches the forest, or scars the fragile Arizona desert with his big, bad 4x4 monster truck. "No man is an island," writes David Watson. "Our lives are woven together, so that who we are and what we do always influences other people. The New Testament knows nothing of the solitary Christian."[2]

## MARRIAGE MYTHS

Right up there with gender stereotypes are marriage myths. Life-bending lies. Paul wrote to the Romans, "They exchanged the truth of God for a lie" (1:25). Now Paul was not thinking specifically about marriage when he wrote this, but the principle applies here. When you reject truth as God has revealed it, you have to make something up. You know, when the kid's caught with a hand in the candy jar, gotta think of somethin'. Gotta think of somethin' fast!

When Moses came down from Mount Sinai with the Ten Commandment engravings in his hands, he was stunned to find the Hebrews reveling in worship to a golden calf. Asking his number two guy, Aaron, what the ruckus was all about, Aaron replied with utter innocence, "Do not be angry, my lord. You know how prone these people are to evil." [Not my fault!] "They said to me, 'Make us gods who will go before us.'" [Still not my fault!]

"So I told them, 'Whoever has any gold jewelry, take it off.' Then they gave me the gold, and I threw it into the fire, *and out came this calf!*" (Exodus 32:21-24).

Well, whadya know? I wonder how *that* happened.

Gotta make somethin' up. Gotta exchange the truth of God for a lie.

Like this: "And they lived happily ever after."

I heard someone say that "they lived happily ever after" is one of the most tragic sentences in literature. It's tragic because it's a falsehood. It is a myth that has led generations to expect something from marriage that is not possible.

But every TV show we watch, every movie, perpetuates this lie. Another couple, Tim and Jill on "Home Improvement," solve life's most difficult problems in just thirty minutes. And they do it with humor and style.

"Seinfeld," on the other hand, solves nothing. The message of this show is that life makes no sense, but everything in the end will be hilariously OK.

Bill Pullman, playing the President of the United States in *Independence Day*, saves the whole world from a mega-invasion in a *couple hours*. And his grief for his dead wife lasts only a couple minutes and is flushed away in the intoxication of his cosmic victory. I mean, a man's gotta do what a man's gotta do.

*Every* show, *every* motion picture is a world beater. That's why we like 'em. Deep inside we wish life were that way, but it's a lie! Entertaining? You bet! Anything real here about how to solve real problems? Nothin' much at all.

In a marvelous book, *Saving Your Marriage Before It Starts*, husband-and-wife authors Les and Leslie Parrott devote an entire chapter—their first chapter—to facing the myths of marriage with honesty.

"The belief in a happily-ever-after-marriage," they write, "is one of the most widely held and destructive marriage myths. But it is only the tip of the marital-myth iceberg. Every difficult marriage is plagued by a vast assortment of misconceptions about what marriage should be."[3]

The Parrotts identify four common myths:

We expect exactly the same things from marriage.

Everything good in our relationship will get better.

Everything bad in my life will eventually disappear.

My spouse will make me whole.

*Saving Your Marriage* also includes a list of unspoken rules we pick up here and there. While these "codes of conduct" are neither inherently harmful or sinful, they can become a source of tension and marital discord if they are not discussed openly. Examples include:

- Don't ask for help unless you are desperate.
- Downplay your successes.
- Don't ever talk about money in public.
- Never call attention to yourself.
- Don't volunteer to help.
- Don't work too long or too hard.
- Don't get sick.
- Never raise your voice.
- Don't talk about your body.
- Clean the kitchen before you go to bed.

- Don't talk about your feelings.
- Don't drive too fast.
- Never buy dessert at a restaurant.
- Don't be so serious.
- Don't buy expensive gifts.

Can you think of any in your own relationship, David and Jill?

Unconscious rules are closely related to unconscious roles, like men should do this and women should do that. The Parrotts list a few of the more common roles husbands and wives play:

- the planner
- the navigator
- the shopper
- the secret-keeper
- the cook
- the comedian
- the gift-buyer
- the cleaner

"If you are like most couples," the Parrotts observe, "you will try to follow a script that was written by the role models you grew up with. Being aware of this natural tendency is often all it takes to save you from a disappointing drama. Once you are aware of the roles you each tend to take, you can then discuss how to write a new script together."[4]

### EXTREME LOVE IS GENDERLESS

I admit, there are differences between men and women. A best seller is *His Needs, Her Needs*, which we happen to be using right now as a "textbook" in our young couples ministry. Another best-selling book, *Men Are from Mars, Women Are from Venus*, is popular outside Christian circles. But in the end, love, as the cohesive power of your family, will always outdistance roles and rules.

The Bible also makes a case for order in the Christian home: "the husband is the head of the wife just as Christ is the head of the church" (Ephesians 5:23). But I've come to the conclusion that sacrificial love and mutual submission to one another is an even higher principle. Ah, but what about 1 Peter 3—"Wives, in the same way *be submissive* to your husbands.... For this is the way of the holy women of the past.... They were submissive to their own husbands, like Sarah, who obeyed Abraham and called him her master" (vv. 15-6).

What do you think, Jill? Is it "biblical" to call David, "Master"?

Hello, Jill. Are you still there?

Let me help you. Actually, the most important words in the entire passage are not "be submissive," but "in the same way." In the same way as what? Look back at 1 Peter 2:21-23: in the same way as Jesus: "To this you were called, because Christ suffered for you, leaving you an example, that you should follow in his steps.... When they hurled their insults at him, he did not retaliate; when he suffered, he made no threats. Instead, he entrusted himself to him who judges justly."

It's in this context that Peter commands, "Wives, *in the same way* be submissive to your husbands"—in the same way as Jesus was submissive to God working through the difficult circumstances of his life. And not to be thought of as a chauvinist, Peter adds later, "Husbands, *in the same way* be considerate as you live with your wives, and treat them with respect" (v. 7).

This passage in the Bible, then, is not mainly about women submitting to men, but *everyone* living *in the same way* as Jesus! A favorite Christian leader of mine, Doug Murren, in his book *Is It Real When It Doesn't Work*, writes, "Christians love without control. *Submission* here is not used in the controlling sense.

Submission is a sensitive process of our listening, hearing, and respecting one another."[5]

Do you care who washes the dishes? Is it a woman's job, or a man's job? Does it really matter? Does it really matter to God?

I don't think so.

God doesn't care about who washes the dishes. Or who fixes the car. Or who reconciles the checkbook with the bank statement. Or even who's in charge.

God the Father is looking for evidence of his Son—in our homes, in our hearts, in our attitudes. *God is not really concerned about who's right. He's concerned about who has the right attitude.*

David and Jill, can you submit to one another out of reverence for Christ, because he is Lord of your marriage?

## "ONE," BUT NOT THE SAME

Marriage is a microcosm in an ecosystem of interdependence, a little planet wild with life in a solar system of interconnected diversity. In 1 Corinthians 12, Paul uses the image of the body of Christ to elaborate on the principle of interdependence. I've identified five important lessons in this passage.

*First, individuality and community are valued equally in God's plan:* "The body is a unit, though it is made up of many parts; and though all its parts are many, they form one body. So it is with Christ" (v. 12).

In American culture, we usually value the individual at the expense of the community. In the old Soviet culture, the community (the State) was valued and protected; the individual was expendable. In the Bible, the individual and the community coexist in purposeful tension. The uniqueness of each individual means nothing without the backdrop of the community, and the community means nothing without the sum diversity of all the individuals!

*Second, God's plan is to make us one without making us the same—and without taking away any individual differences:* "For we were all baptized by *one* Spirit into *one* body" (v. 13).

David and Jill, when I pronounced you husband-and-wife, you became *one* in spirit, and on your honeymoon you became *one* flesh. *One!* But not *the same!* No one asked me at your reception, "Now tell me again, which one is the bride and which one is the groom? They look so much alike!"

When you were married, David and Jill, God made you *one* without taking away what makes each of you so special—and the differences will not go away. Ever! In some ways, they will become even more pronounced!

Deal with it!

*Third, God made us different on purpose:* "Now the body is not made up of one part but of many…. If the whole body were an eye, where would the sense of hearing be? If the whole body were an ear, where would the sense of smell be?" (vv. 14, 17). Every person is unique, and each person's uniqueness is God's gift to everyone else. From another perspective, what we don't like about the other person (about our spouse?) is just as much a part of God's plan as what we like about them, which leads me to my *fourth* observation…

*Fourth, nothing about your relationship is accidental:* "But in fact God has arranged the parts in the body, every one of them, just as he wanted" (v. 18). This means, I'm quite sure, that we can't take anything in any relationship for granted, because somehow God is in it, good and bad, blessing and pain, *for better or for worse,* for richer or for poorer, in sickness and in health.

## NO CONTROL OVER THE IN-LAWS

Think about it. Really … do you have any control over the relationships of your life? Yes, David and Jill, you had some control in choosing each other, in that you could decide whether or not to marry. But Jill, you couldn't choose your in-laws! You may have chosen David, but you may or may not have cared for David's entire network of family and friends.

You can choose where to work, but you can't choose who will be working with you. Someday you will choose to have children, but you can't choose what your children will be like. It's all in the hands of God! He "has arranged the parts in the body, every one of them, just as he wanted them to be."

But what about terrible things that happen, like sexual and physical abuse? No, I didn't say God *causes* everything to happen, but God can turn the worst things that happen to good for those who love God.

If you don't believe that, then faith in Christ is only good when life is good, but the Bible promises that "in *all these things* (yes, *all*) we are *more* than conquerors through him who loved us" (Romans 8:37). Yes, I can endure "*everything* through [Christ] who gives me strength" (Philippians 4:13).

*Fifth, the people we think we need the least, we need the most*: "The eye cannot say to the hand, 'I don't need you!' And the head cannot say to the feet, 'I don't need you'" (v. 21).

Now remember, Paul isn't just teaching anatomy here. No, he's writing to Christians in the Corinthian community who were shamefully severed into feuding factions. And you know what people were saying? "I don't need that person in my life."

I've said that.

David, do you remember my personal year of hell in 1987? Our church exploded in misunderstanding and betrayal. "I don't need this in my life," I kept saying.

Looking back, however, I'm gripped by a supernatural sense of gratefulness for what happened to me at that time. Without that pain, I could not be the person I am today, and God knew that. I've settled it in my mind that the people I thought I needed least, I needed the most.

David and Jill, can you *value* difference in each other? No, I didn't say, "Can you *tolerate* difference." Tolerance, you know, is politically correct. Live and let live, they say. But for the Christian believer, tolerance is a mere shadow of the love of God that *values* difference and believes that somehow, someway, God is in everything for good.

## THE LITTLE WAY

I'd like to wrap up this chapter with a story of "The Little Way of Thérèse of Lisieux" told by best-selling Christian writer Richard Foster. "This simple woman," he writes, "known only as 'the Little Flower,' devised a prayer-filled approach to life that has helped many. This Little Way, as she called it, is deceptively simple. It is, in short, to seek out the menial job, to welcome unjust criticisms, *to befriend those who annoy us,* to help those who are ungrateful....

"An incident from Thérèse's autobiography, *The Story of a Soul,* underscores the hiddenness of the Little Way. One uneducated and rather conceited sister had managed to irritate Thérèse in everything she did. Rather than avoid this person, however, she took the Little Way straight into the conflict: 'I set myself to treat her as if I loved her best of all.' Thérèse succeeded so well in her Little Way that following her death this same sister declared, 'During her life, I made her really happy.'"[6]

David and Jill, submit to one another out of reverence for Christ and do whatever you can to serve each other and others in all kinds of little ways every day. Extreme love is larger than gender stereotypes and irreconcilable differences.

---

**AND IN THE NEXT CHAPTER, HOW TO**
**MAKE CONFIDENT DECISIONS IN A**
**COMPLEX WORLD.**

---

FIVE

---

## WHAT TO DO?

---

*How to make confident decisions
in a complex world*

Dave, do you remember how you decided to attend Biola University?

You were looking at about five different colleges—and you wanted to do the right thing. Even more, you really wanted *your* choice to be *God's* choice.

What to do?

We talked about a lot of different factors, but two considerations really helped you make the final decision: first, Biola offered you more scholarship money than anybody else, and second, Jill was already attending Pacific Christian College just eight miles from Biola.

Generous scholarships and Jill! Biola had to be the will of God for your life!

At least it seemed that way at the time, and looking back five years later, we all would agree that it was absolutely the right decision because everything seemed to work out so well. You could not have had a better four years at any college, and now you're working for Barna Research, and you love that too.

Maybe that wouldn't have happened if you had not attended college in Southern California.

Yeah, it was a good decision.

Your decision to marry each other seemed very right, too, but I remember you both had some doubts after a couple years of dating. You were mature enough to realize that life-making decisions have huge repercussions—especially the decision to get married!

## TOO MANY CHOICES

Remember when I spoke about decision-making at the student chapel at Biola? I began my little talk by presenting a plaque I had picked up in Australia to your sister Shari, right in front of all her friends. It said:

> *I used to be indecisive,*
> *but now I'm not so sure.*

Why are we so indecisive? Why are decisions so difficult? And why is it so easy to make the wrong choice? I think there are at least three reasons.

*1. There are just too many choices.* We live in an age of over-choice, another word we get from the famed Alvin Toffler's *Future Shock.*

There are examples of overchoice everywhere, like cable TV. I mean, how many channels do we really need?

Or video stores. We've done it together. Stood there in a stupor, numbed by the vast selection of videos.

After my friend Max and I spent an exhausting hour at a Blockbuster Video a few months ago, we finally yielded to our inveterate indecision and drove home without a movie.

What to do?

What to do on the Internet? Where to eat, and what to eat when you get there? Where to shop at the mega-mall and then what to buy?

CEREAL CHOICE OVERLOAD

You know I haven't done a lot of grocery shopping through the years, so when Mom sends me to the store for bread, she has to call in search-and-rescue to find me and get me home. I mean, the typical bread aisle is as long as half a football field. (Sorry, Jill, about the football field. It's a guy thing.)

And cars. Twenty-five years ago Alvin Toffler cited a study of overchoice in the automobile industry. Way back then someone sat down at his primitive computer and put all of the variations available in automobiles—body styles, colors, accessories—into his system.

After the computer groaned and blinked for a few seconds, it revealed this startling finding: American consumers could choose from some twenty-five million different automobiles. And picking which car to buy is easy compared to some decisions.[1] We live in an age of overchoice.

*2. Another reason why it's so tough to make good decisions is, well, sin.* By sin, I don't just mean the worst imaginable evil, but "doing it my own way," as Solomon warned: "There is a way that *seems* right to a man, but in the end it leads to death" (Proverbs 14:12).

There are lots of ways to do it my way—*selfishly.*

Out of my emotions, not my head.

In a hurry, in a panic. Impulsively. As fast as I can, without stopping to consider the consequences of my decision.

Willfully, without listening to the advice of those who probably know better.

Absolutely convinced I'm right, against the best advice of others.

*3. No two decisions are the same.* In other words, not only are there too many choices, but every choice, every decision, is unique. Dave and Jill, the decisions you make will range from simple to complex, from moral, to sort of moral, to amoral.

M. Blaine Smith, in his excellent book *Knowing God's Will:*

*Finding Guidance for Personal Decisions* (I recommend it!) identifies different kinds of decisions. *First, there are straightforward moral decisions.* The Ten Commandments are examples. In other words, you don't have to stop and think about what you should do whenever a choice is clearly moral or immoral.

Less people than ever say they believe in absolute truth. Haven't you found at Barna Research that 70 percent or more *don't* believe it? We have become a sand-castle culture of marriages and families without moral values.

But Christians ought to believe, need to believe, must believe that some things are just plain right, others are just plain wrong, and God's laws must guide every decision we make: "These words I speak to you," Jesus announced, "are not incidental additions to your life, homeowner improvements to your standard of living. They are foundational words, words to build a life on. If you work these words into your life, you are like a smart carpenter who built his house on a solid rock. Rain poured down, the river flooded, a tornado hit—but nothing moved that house. It was fixed to the rock.

"But if you just use my words in Bible studies and don't work them into your life, you are like a stupid carpenter who built his house on the sandy beach. When a storm rolled in and the waves came up, it collapsed like a house of cards" (Matthew 7:24-27, *The Message*).

*A second decision-making category: complicated moral decisions.* Some Christian people would like to think that *everything* is clearly right or wrong. But you need to know this, David and Jill, *most of the decisions of life are not black and white, but gray.* Many are dark gray.

Abortion is an example.

Wait a minute! Isn't abortion clearly wrong?

Yes! But what about in the case of incest? Or rape? Do you have an easy answer for that?

Should Christians go to war?

Should Christians go to court?

An extraordinary example of a complex moral decision is found in 2 Kings 5:9-19, the account of Naaman the leper.

"Go bathe seven times in the Jordan River," the prophet Elisha commanded him.

At first, Naaman refused, but later submitted to the better judgment of his aide—and he was miraculously cured. Most everyone who has spent any time in Sunday School has heard the story. Most of it. The end is less familiar: "But may the Lord forgive your servant for this one thing," Naaman confessed to Elijah. "When my master enters the temple of the pagan god Rimmon to bow down, and he is leaning on my arm, and I bow there also—when I bow down in the temple of the pagan god Rimmon, may the Lord forgive your servant for this."

"Go in peace," Elisha.

Amazing! Elisha said it was OK to bow down to a pagan god!

Actually, it's more like amazing grace. Elisha, the great prophet of Jehovah, the God of Mount Sinai, allowed a moral concession—at least it seems like that—in Naaman's unusual situation.

This is one of those complex moral decisions. In seminary, in government, in medicine, it's called ethics—a careful consideration of questions of right and wrong when there is no clear right and wrong. *Every* complex moral decision is just that: *complex.*

## AND ... NOW ... FOR THE MOST DIFFICULT KIND OF DECISION

*Third, many decisions are non-moral, but they're still complex.* Your choice of college, Dave, is an example. Yes, it was a fairly straightforward decision for you, but for your sister, the choice was more complex—and painful. Although she finally committed to Biola University as well, she had an offer-she-couldn'trefuse from another school. Well, she refused, and the process of coming to a final decision was difficult and emotional.

M. Blaine Smith writes insightfully about this: "In general, questions such as these cannot be resolved simply by applying moral principles to them. In most cases we are left with a good deal of freedom of choice…. This is the area of decision making that usually causes the most difficulty and where we most often experience confusion over God's will."[2]

Do you understand why he comes to that conclusion? Do you grasp the full implications of his statement? He is saying, in effect, that some of the most important decisions in life, like where to attend college, where to live, where to work, and even whom to marry, cannot be placed squarely in or out of the will of God—because they are decisions which are essentially amoral.

In other words, there's no Bible verse to tell you if it's right for you to live and work in California and wrong for you to live and work in Arizona. Not every decision is a "Christian choice" or a "non-Christian choice."

Many decisions are complex because *life is complex!*

*Fourth, the great majority of decisions we make are straightforward, nonmoral decisions.* Like what to cook for dinner, or whether or not to eat out, or what to order when you eat out, or what to do on your day off. According to one study conducted by Dr. Erich Klinger at the University of Minnesota, each of us faces—I know this is hard to believe—between three hundred and seventeen thousand decisions *every day!* Most of these are straightforward, nonmoral decisions.

Well, enough about different kinds of decisions. How about some advice on how to go about making good decisions? I have come up with a personal list of five things you need to know when making complex decisions. And Dave and Jill, I even suggest that you use this list as a checkpoint from time to time when you are faced with the more far-reaching decisions of your life.

*First*—and this should be obvious by now!—*don't ever, ever make a plainly immoral decision.* "Your word," King David professed in Psalm 119:105, "is a lamp to my feet and a light for my path."

In moral issues there is only one right choice: obedience to God's word, no matter what the consequences. And there is only one way to make decisions: with a godly heart. "We are to act in love and kindness," writes Haddon Robinson. "We are to have integrity. We are to be faithful and generous. And we are to operate out of proper motives."[3]

## WHAT'S GOD'S WILL FOR OUR LIVES?

Dave and Jill, I couldn't tell you how many times I've been asked to pray for God's will for someone's life, usually about a relationship, a job, or a move. But God's will is *primarily* about who you *are* and *how you do what you do*, and *secondarily* about *what* you do. Paul believed this too: "Make sure that nobody pays back wrong for wrong, but always try to be kind to each other and to everyone else. Be joyful always; pray continually; give thanks in all circumstances, *for this is God's will for you*" (1 Thessalonians 5:15-18).

Sometimes I think that when people say they want to know God's will about a relationship, a job, or a move, what they really mean is that they don't want to make a "wrong" decision, one they will regret someday—a decision that will in some way make them unhappy. We're more concerned about our *future* than we are about our *character.*

I know this flies in the face of popular Christian opinion, but what matters so much to us, doesn't matter so much to God. In fact, I'm convinced that God has given us far more freedom of choice than we are willing to give ourselves, which leads me to my second principle....

*Second, love God and do whatever you want* (thanks to St.

Augustine for this one). I know I'm opening one can of worms after another, but *not everything in life is predetermined.*

Yes, God has a plan for me, for you. But his plan is more about my inner life and how I serve others than whether I'm a doctor or a nurse, a pastor or a plumber.

God guides us, but many of the choices we make set the course of our lives and the lives of others, and what God cares about is how we behave ourselves on the journey. Another way to say this is that God is interested in the process as much as in the goal. We're not just *going* somewhere, we're *growing* somewhere. Life is *not* a series of carefully sequenced, predetermined events, but the unfolding of a relationship with God in our hearts.

### PLAYING "BATTLESHIP" WITH GOD

For many Christians, prayer and finding God's will are like playing Battleship with God. You know how to play this game, Dave, but I have to explain it for everybody else who is reading our personal mail: two players mark the location of their ships on a grid of numbered vertical columns and lettered horizontal columns. The object of the game is to locate your opponent's ships by randomly calling out squares on the grid, like A-12, or C-5.

And that's how we try to find God will.

I start: "OK, God, let's try … B-11."

"**MISS,**" shouts a loud voice from heaven.

"Ah, er … D-4."

"**MISS AGAIN.**"

"OK, how about E-1."

"**AH, ALMOST. I HAD MY SHIP THERE A MINUTE AGO, BUT YOU KNOW, I'M GOD. I GET**

## TO MOVE MY SHIPS AROUND."

*Grrrrrrr!* Yes, I'm growling in my heart. "Well then, maybe ("maybe" means my faith is getting weak) ... E-2."

**SILENCE.**

"God, I said E-2."

Still **SILENCE.**

Now I'm *really* frustrated: "God, maybe we should do this again tomorrow."

🤱 🤱 🤱

No one is so stupid as to think that prayer is like Battleship, but that's the way a lot of Christians think about finding the will of God, that everything is carefully predetermined and our goal is to figure out what God has planned.

Go figure.

We know, of course, we could only be *happy* (there's that word again) if we are doing *exactly* what God wants.

Problem is, if he exactly wants this or that, why doesn't he exactly tell us?

The answer is—back to my main point—because God has given us a great degree of freedom in making choices.

### GOD ISN'T GOOFY, WE ARE

Imagine, Dave, if I raised you the way we presume God raises us. Picture your mother and me before you were born, sitting down together and plotting the course of your life. All of it, down to every hour of every day, written on a secret calendar.

But we don't tell you what we've written down. You have to figure it out. When you do, Mom and I get real happy. We smile. We laugh. We pat you on the back. We double your allowance.

*But when you don't* ... We scowl. We frown. We take away your breakfast.

Does that sound ludicrous, or what? Yet that's how so many people relate to God. It's so sad.

When I raised you kids, I gave you guidance, sometimes forcefully! But most of the time, Mom and I didn't tell you exactly what to do in every little decision in your life. In fact, the older you got, the less exactly we guided you. My goal was not to tell you what to do, so you would never have a mind of your own, but to teach you to do whatever you do in a godly way.

If everything were predetermined, there would be no need for God to warn me in the Bible about the consequences of my wrong choices and decisions. The very fact that the Bible is full of warnings presupposes that we have the responsibility to make choices, hopefully the right ones.

*Guidance is not just figuring out what God is planning for my future, but making the right decisions, according to the wise principles of God's Word, that will lead me into my future.* God doesn't always tell me specifically what I am to do with my life, but he does tell me that wherever I go, he will go with me. In fact (Can you believe this?), he is even there by my side when I make wrong decisions! Like I've been there for you kids, even when you did wrong things.

There's a famous Bible verse about this: "The Lord is my shepherd, I shall not be in want.... He guides me in the paths of righteousness for his name's sake" (Psalm 23:1, 3). "For his name's sake" suggests he has a vested interest in what happens to us, not unlike my interest as a dad in what happens to you. In a curious sort of way, your success is my success, and I agonize with you in your failures and pain.

## COUNTING SHEEP

Some years ago I had a dream-like experience in the pine-forested mountains of northern Arizona. I was doing a personal prayer retreat at your grandparents' cabin. Deciding I needed to get some fresh mountain air late in the day, I took a short drive on a dusty, gravel road into the forest. The late afternoon sun filtered through the pines, backlighting the small groves of western oak and illuminating the leaves golden green like a million Christmas lights. Spattered sunlight was flickering on my windshield.

What happened next was surreal. As I rounded a bend, there in front of me crossing the road were a hundred or more sheep, each one haloed in shimmering, golden wool as the setting sun gleamed behind them. It was magical and entirely unexpected. I've lived in Arizona for forty years and didn't have a clue that sheep in great numbers graze in our Ponderosa forests.

Forced to stop the car, I stepped out onto the gravel road and shouted, "This is soooo beautiful," not realizing that a shepherd—a *real* shepherd—was standing just off the road. Watching. Watching the sheep. Watching me act like a jerk. My moment of ecstasy was his daily misery.

What really hit me in that heaven-like moment was how the sheep—some feeding on either side of the road, some crossing, some just standing there—were hardly aware of the shepherd. Each animal was going about its own business, each with a range of personal freedom.

*The Lord is my Shepherd....*
*I will fear no evil, for you are with me;*
*your rod and your staff, they comfort me.*

The shepherd was watching and guiding, but the sheep were making a lot of their own decisions—within the circle of his will. As a father to you kids, like a shepherd, I was watching and guiding, but you had to make a lot of your own decisions—within the circle of my will.

Life leaves me feeling so helpless at times. And fearful about many of the decisions I have to make. But the Lord is my Shepherd. He leads me when I don't know where I'm going—

and protects me, not just from animals of prey, but from the consequences of my own stupidity.

This is why St. Augustine could say confidently, "Love God and do whatever you want." There's a Bible verse about this too, where Nathan, King David's personal spiritual counselor, encouraged David, "Whatever you have in mind, go ahead and do it, for the Lord is with you" (2 Samuel 7:3).

"How can you know with certainty that you are doing the will of God?" someone once asked Mother Teresa.

"I *am* the will of God," she responded.

Wow! Whether or not she's doing the "right" thing apparently never enters her mind. She just loves God and expects that everything else is going to work out somehow. Oh yeah, Romans 8:28 *does* say that, doesn't it? "We know that to those who love God, who are called according to his plan, everything that happens fits into a pattern for God" (J.B. Phillips).

## INDY RACING FOR GOD

Well, remember, I've been sharing with you five things you need to know when making complex decisions. The *third* is this: *recognize and accept your own personal gifts and limitations.* In other words, ask yourself, "What do I (we) *like* to do?"

This overturns another Christian myth, the myth that God will only ask you do to something you don't like to do, just to see if you really love him. Or, if you like to do something, God must not be in it.

But that's as goofy as playing battleship with God. Think about it. Why would God bother to create you one way, put all kinds of legitimate likes and dislikes in your heart, and then tell you to do something with your life that doesn't fit how he created you?

I am persuaded otherwise. God generally will lead you in the direction of what you like, what you enjoy. Oh, there will be exceptions. You're not going to like everything about your life, and you will have to do unpleasant things, but God is on your side. God isn't weird, people are.

Different motor vehicles, for example, are designed and constructed for different purposes. Imagine again, if you will, that God created you to be a UPS truck, but you have this feeling that just to test your faith and to build your character, God wants you racing in the Indianapolis 500.

There you go, as fast as you can. As fast as your big, bad, bulky body will carry you.

Screaming by in a blur of color and speed are the sleek Indy cars.

*YEEEEEEEEEEERM! YEEEEEEEEEEEERM!*

It's so embarrassing, but you're doing it for God, and he's so proud of you. You even have a shiny fish emblem on your big, brown back door to let others know you're doin' it for God.

(I was telling this story at a Youth With A Mission discipleship school in Denver, and right then, no joke, a UPS truck pulled up outside the giant picture window on the right side of the classroom.)

Again, the myth is that God made you one way, but forces you to do something incompatible with your gifts and interests. The truth is that God uses you the way he made you. One of the greatest preachers of the nineteenth century, Charles Spurgeon, once said, "If you cannot speak in public, then God has not called you to preach."

Don't dream about doing something you're not gifted to do, and don't feel guilty doing something you like. *Acknowledging and accepting your gifts and limitations will help you make right decisions.*

## CIRCUMSTANTIAL EVIDENCE

The *fourth* thing you need to know to make good decisions in a complex world is, and this one is easy, *just consider the circumstances.* In other words, make a list of the pros and cons.

Circumstances fall into two simple categories: constraining and non-constraining. I like what Christian writer M. Blaine Smith has to say about this: "There are two basic principles which can reduce our confusion and make it easier to recognize God's leading [in circumstances]....

"In a *major* decision (a decision for a vocation, for example), circumstances should play only a limited role in discerning God's will. At best, we should let them play either a *suggestive* or *confirming* role....

"In the area of minor decisions (that is, decisions *within* a vocation for example), we should see circumstances as playing a much more defined role."

*Fifth* thing you should know: *Get counsel.* The Old Testament book of Proverbs says a lot about this:

"The way of a fool seems right to him, but a wise man listens to advice" (12:15).

"Plans fail for lack of counsel, but with many advisers they succeed" (15:22).

"Listen to advice and accept instruction, and in the end you will be wise" (19:20).

"The purposes of a man's heart are deep waters, but a man of understanding draws them out" (20:5).

Haddon Robinson, in his book *Decision Making by the Book,* tells us that we need to seek counsel that contains three important elements. Good counsel is:

- *Biblical.* When we are seeking God's will, we need the advice of someone with a Christian world view.
- *Experienced.* The counselor should be someone who is mature and who has the big picture.

- *Skilled.* The counselor should be someone who is knowledgeable in the area in which you need advice, for example brain surgery. I'd rather get the counsel of the best surgeon in the world *regardless* of whether he or she is a Christian![4]

## I WOULD LIKE TO BE DONE WITH THIS CHAPTER, BUT...

*The second to the last thing:* What if you make a wrong decision? A good neighbor remarked to me once, "We've taught our children that you have to make decisions on the best information you have at the time, and then once you decide, don't look back."

Good advice! And I'm not even sure if these people were Christian believers!

Well, but what if the decision is a bad one?

*Admit your mistake.* It's OK. Everyone makes mistakes. Everyone makes stupid decisions. You'll never learn how to succeed unless you first learn how to fail.

Failure to come clean about your failure will, however, just prolong the agony. Problems drag on and on because somebody just can't say, "I made a big mistake. I'm really sorry. Forgive me. I've learned my lesson, and God helping me, I won't do this again."

Or even, "I have a big problem here. I need help. I'm going to take these action steps to change."

*Accept the consequences of bad decisions.* Sometimes the consequences are serious and painful, but denying your mistakes is much worse in the end. You have to learn to live with failure realistically. God isn't blown away by your failures, but he is concerned about how you handle them.

*Don't assume every decision is forever.* Sometimes the only thing that's permanent is our egos! Make new decisions. Changing your mind is not schizophrenic!

*Resist with all your might the compelling temptation to correct a bad decision with another impulsive, bad decision.* The pain people bring on themselves by their own bad decisions is staggering, but the self-deceiving things they do to compensate for their bad decisions may be even worse. Take King David, for example. Adultery with Bathsheba wasn't enough; he had to have her husband killed to cover his sin when he got her pregnant.

Never forget: things will always go from bad to worse until you do the right thing.

*And the last thing:* What do I do when I absolutely don't know what to do? The answer is really simple: *Set a time limit.* You can't stand on the crossroads of indecision forever! You gotta do something!

I've given this advice to countless people—with good results. Here's how it works. When you're stuck, when you know there will be something to lose no matter what you choose, take the best information you have and decide to do *something* on a predetermined date—in three months, let's say, or in thirty days.

If your decision involves a difficult relationship with someone, don't tell them what you've decided, or the date you've chosen. That would be terribly manipulative. Just tell God and then pray, believing that he will make it obvious in some way that what you decided is not best. It's like telling God, "This is what I'm going to do, and I'm going to do it by January 1. But if this is a bad idea, make it plain to me otherwise."

You understand, of course, that this approach to making a tough decision is rooted in what I believe about God: he is the Good Shepherd, not some tricky deity who keeps changing the rules in the middle of the game. *God is on your side.*

God is not just concerned about your making the *right* decision. He is concerned about your making every decision *the right way.* God is not just waiting to see what you are going to do, but *how* you are going to do it. If you make the *right* decision with the *wrong* attitude, you have made the wrong decision! But if you make the *wrong* decision with the *right* attitude, God will intervene.

*Fear not!* When you set a time limit, you're not testing God, or putting God on the spot. You're putting *you* on the spot! Don't stand there forever! For heaven's sake, make up your mind! If you wait too long, *no decision* will be the *right decision*!

*Fear not!* If you know exactly what you're supposed to do in advance, you wouldn't need any faith! Why? Because faith is the evidence of things *not seen* (Hebrews 11:1). *Faith is a calculated risk!*

It takes no faith to make a decision when you already know exactly what's going to happen. Faith always implies a measure of uncertainty. Where there is no uncertainty, there is no faith.

"It is better to be right 50 percent of the time," says Haddon Robinson, "and get something done than it is to get nothing done because you are afraid to be wrong."[5]

---

**AND IN THE NEXT CHAPTER ... HOW DO YOU**

**GET THE MOST OUT OF YOUR JOB?**

---

## SIX

# THANK GOD IT'S MONDAY

*Making the most of your job*

I hardly ever miss a day of reading the newspaper.
Now Jill, don't just think it's about the sports page.
There's so much other thoughtful news and information, and you know I love to collect things. Like headlines:

"Dwindling manners lead to rage in the office cage."
"Desk drummers, change jinglers jangle nerves: Co-workers' quirks top survey of pet peeves."
"On-job stress is making workers sick."
"Stressed workers filling doctors' waiting rooms."
"Companies try to help employees cope."
"Women making progress in workplace, but glass ceiling still exists."

According to one of these articles, the American Medical Association estimates that up to 70 percent of all patients seen by general-practice physicians come with symptoms directly related to unrelieved stress. And stress all by itself—as in "I'm stressed"—is among the top ten reasons Americans miss work.

What's even worse, Patterson and Kim, authors of the popular book *The Day America Told the Truth*, report that only one in ten Americans say they are satisfied with their work, and only one in four employees gives his or her best effort on the job, and that about 20 percent of the average worker's time is wasted.

## WORK ON YOUR MARRIAGE

Do you feel the same way about your jobs, David and Jill? Some of the time? Most of the time?

Well, maybe you both actually like your work! But you've only been married a year (a year today as I write this!), and Jill, you've already talked with me a couple times about David bringing his work home. Is that distressing?

Even more potentially hurtful to your marriage are those times you bring home your *feelings* about work *with* your work.

Here's what happens: You're stressed at work. You can't deal with it there. You gotta stuff it.

You come home from work, genuinely glad to see each other. You're looking for that first welcome-home kiss. Inside, however, you're combative, bristling.

Then something happens and you're over the edge. Now you're angry with one another. For nothin'. At first it had everything to do with work and nothing to do with each other, but not anymore.

Been there. Mom and I have had our worst fights when I'm having my worst weeks at work. I've seen it with Mom, too, when her "job" was raising you kids. And more recently, she has been more noticeably stressed as a result of taking a part-time job.

Pressure at work brings added pressure to our relationship, so what we might tolerate in one another at any other time without a burp of anger, suddenly becomes a point of serious conflict. If you think that what you're thinking and feeling about work *isn't* affecting your marriage, you're dreamin'. There's a direct relationship between work and marriage.

CALENDAR WITH AN ATTITUDE

## CURSE ON WORK

Want to know why most people—as in 90 percent of the American workforce—are so stressed and unhappy about their jobs? *Because there's a curse on work.*

That's why Christian author R. Kent Hughes writes, "Millions of people regard their work as something they must bear, a living indignity…. A dark cloud of dissatisfaction blankets today's workforce."

… and why Herman Melville, author of the classic novel *Moby Dick*, wrote, "They talk of dignity of work, bosh! The dignity is in the leisure."

… and why secular, best-selling author Studs Terkel, in his book *Working*, concedes, "Work is about violence—to the spirit as well as to the body. It is about ulcers as well as accidents. About shouting matches as well as fist fights. About nervous breakdowns as well as kicking the dog around. It is, above (or beneath) all, about daily humiliations."[1]

You don't have to be a theologian to recognize that *there's a curse on work.*

God said to Adam, "Because you listened to your wife [Don't get the wrong message from this, Dave] and ate from the tree about which I commanded you, 'You must not eat of it,' *Cursed is the ground because of you*; through painful toil you will eat of it all the days of your life. It will produce thorns and thistles for you, and you will eat the plants of the field. By the sweat of your brow you will eat your food until you return to the ground" (Genesis 3:17-19).

I know … lots of people would not be real happy about my "religious" explanation of the problem. In fact, none of the articles I listed at the beginning of this chapter, as you would expect, says anything about God or spirituality. (Those subjects appear only once a week, Saturday, and are hidden on the religion page in Section D.)

In one of those reports on work and the workplace, the newspaper included a side bar—tips from the HOPE Heart Institute on handling stress, including some really good recommendations, like:

organized
the present
others
ıgh
ɔ their own thing
ᵗ a break
Moni                              goes on in your head
ᶠ right
vords
ıngry

Conspicuously                        though, is anything spiritual, yet I am con                    ɔf the problem is how we understand our wc                    God. To put it another way, the curse on w                    ᶦGod in the workplace. God has stepped ou                    , ɩɩot for a few minutes, but forever. The workplac ɩɩas become godless.

The ultimate curse, of course, is hell, which is the absolute absence of God. Wherever you have the absolute absence of God you have absolute hell, and when you have a godless workplace, your job is going to feel like hell.

In a new publication, *The Kingdom Agenda*, Mike Rogers and Claude King compare the workplace God intended with the one sin corrupted:

**What God intended...**
God and his workers work together.
God is present, and his workers are aware of his presence.
God is sovereign and the workers are cooperative.

God assigns work and his workers respond to God's initiative
in obedience.

*Yeah, right!*

**What it's really like...**
Workers reject God's sovereignty.
Workers focus on themselves.
Workers attempt to satisfy their needs apart from God.[2]

There's a curse on work, and without God work takes
on a life of its own....
It becomes your source of income, so you work for pay.
It becomes your source of meaning, so you work for ful-
fillment.
It becomes your source of identity, so you work for your
success.
It becomes your master, and you become its slave.
*In a godless workplace, work becomes your god.*

### DO YOU HAVE A SECULAR JOB?

When you say, "I have a *secular* (as opposed to *sacred*) job,"
you are fully acknowledging the absence of God in the workplace. Or to say it more bluntly, if you think your job is secular,
you are cursing your work, because the essence of the curse is
the absence of God.

In fact, there is no such thing as secular work, only a secular
*view* of work, which sounds like this:

"The ultimate purpose of my work is to give me a sense of
personal value and fulfillment."
"Success in life means success in my work."

"You can tell how successful I am by my material wealth, my professional recognition, or my positional status."

"I just go to work to earn a living."

"I expect more of work and of myself than work or self can deliver."

"My career, my success, my position, my income is an idol in my life."

"My view of work leaves God out of the system."[3]

## MEANINGLESS, MENIAL WORK

The curse on work isn't just what it does to you, but what happens to human society: your value as a human being is measured not by what's inside of you, but what kind of job you have. We have become enslaved by "status," and "menial work" is something for illiterates and immigrants.

Well, would you look at this! I checked my electronic thesaurus for synonyms of "menial." Here are the words listed:

| | |
|---|---|
| drudge | lowly |
| base | servant |
| domestic (???) | servile |
| hack | subordinate |
| hireling | subservient |
| ignoble | underling |
| lackey | vile |

And the antonyms? Only three:

employer
dignified
executive

Does this support what I'm saying, or what!

The curse on work, inherent in our language, gives work a life of its own, resulting in the isolation and humiliation of social categories.

Solomon wrote some twenty-five hundred years ago, "So I hated life, because the work that is done under the sun was grievous to me. All of it is meaningless, a chasing after the wind. I hated all the things I had toiled for under the sun, because I must leave them to the one who comes after me. And who knows whether he will be a wise man or a fool? Yet he will have control over all the work into which I have poured my effort and skill under the sun. This too is meaningless.

"So my heart began to despair over all my toilsome labor under the sun. For a man may do his work with wisdom, knowledge and skill, and then he must leave all he owns to someone who has not worked for it. This too is meaningless and a great misfortune. What does a man get for all the toil and anxious striving with which he labors under the sun? All his days his work is pain and grief; even at night his mind does not rest.

This too is meaningless," groaned Solomon (Ecclesiastes 2:17-23).

In contrast, consider the patriarch Joseph, one of the twelve sons of Israel. Joseph was a dreamer, dreamed that one day his brothers—his *older* brothers—would bow down to him. Problem was he told his older brothers, and they jumped at the chance to sell him into slavery.

In the providence of God, Joseph ended up in Egypt in the house of Potiphar. "The Lord was with Joseph and he prospered, and he lived in the house of his Egyptian master" (Genesis 39:2). Right there, working a "secular" job, working for a pagan, *the Lord was with Joseph*. And more, *he prospered*.

In fact, "When his master saw that the Lord was with him and that the Lord gave him success in everything he did, Joseph found favor in his eyes and became his attendant" (39:3-4). God blessed his "secular" work and made Joseph successful— every hard working person's dream. Because Joseph was resourceful? No! Because *the Lord was with him*. Remember, the essence of the curse is the *absence* of God. Joseph was blessed because of the *presence* of God.

"From the time he put him charge of his household and of all that he owned, the Lord blessed the household of the Egyptian because of Joseph"(39:5). That's why God gave you your job! To bless the pagan!

Instead of whining (see Chapter 2), be grateful! Acknowledge that your work is spiritual service, even when you're working for unspiritual people. Know that God is with you, like Joseph. If you are a Christian, you have to keep reminding yourself that your *secular* job is really a *full-time ministry* to the people you're working for and with.

Paul wrote to the young man, Titus, "Teach slaves to be subject to their masters in everything, to try to please them, not to talk back to them, and not to steal from them, but to show that they can be fully trusted, so that [I love this part] *in every way they will make the teaching about God our Savior attractive*" (Titus 2:9-10).

How you do your work is one of the most powerful ways you can communicate your faith in Christ to others. On the other hand, do you ever feel sorry for yourself and whimper, "I'm the only one doin' all the work around here. Everyone else is a slacker, and all my boss does is sit around eatin' donuts and drinkin' coffee"?

Well, with Joseph working for him, "the blessing of the Lord was on everything Potiphar had, both in the house and in the field. So he left in Joseph's care everything he had; with Joseph in charge, he did not concern himself with anything *except the food he ate*" (Genesis 39:5-6).

Donuts and coffee.

## THANK GOD IT'S MONDAY

My point is this: *nobody* has a secular job, not even people who are thoroughly secular, because work is spiritual; work is from God. It was his idea in the first place and he was the first to work: "Thus the heavens and the earth were completed in all their vast array. By the seventh day God had finished *the work* he had been doing; so on the seventh day he rested from all *his work* (Genesis 2:1-2).

We look *forward* to the weekend and say, "It is good."

T. G. I. F.

But when God finally made it to the end of the first work week ever, he looked *back* and said, "It is good."

Thank God, it's Monday!

For God, the weekend was not just the long-awaited end of the week, but a time to look back, to reflect on his work, and to value what he had done.

God worked and work was good. Then God made Adam and put him to work *before* the curse: "Now the Lord God had planted a garden in the east, in Eden; and there he put the man he had formed…. The Lord God took the man and put him in the Garden of Eden *to work it* and take care of it" (Genesis 2:8,15).

Work wasn't a curse, isn't a curse. "Menial" work wasn't a curse either. Think about it: the first job ever was gardening— not as a rose-growing hobby, but as a career and a ministry to the new creation order.

Earlier this fall, a friend of mine, Myles Munroe, an author and highly-acclaimed conference speaker, shared in a special weeknight service at our church. The atmosphere was electric, and the place was packed. We had people sitting in the lobby!

Among other things—*many* other things—Myles spoke on work. When he offered a free copy of his book on finding God's purpose in your job, a young man dashed to the front of the church to take it from him. Graciously, Myles handed him the book, but first asked he what he did for a living.

Looking straight down at the church carpet, the young man refused to answer.

### ONION RINGS FOR GOD

"Tell me," Myles insisted.

After a forever of silence, the guy muttered (I couldn't hear him just a few feet away), "I serve fast food."

"You serve fast food?" Myles echoed loudly so everyone could hear. "What's so bad about that?" Myles chided him lovingly. "Don't *ever* be embarrassed about a job! Work is good, and we should be grateful for any job, every job."

And then in an extraordinary moment, waving his hand over the huge crowd, Myles shouted at the young man, *"All these people here tonight eat fast food!"* Then turning toward the crowd he shouted, *"Don't you?"* The crowd burst into loud, self-conscious laughter.

If all legitimate work comes from God, then work is *good*. You might even say it's *sacred*. Or to say it in still another way, work is worship. To work hard and to work well, whatever you do, is to honor God...

whether you deep-fry onion rings or fly airplanes

whether you pump gas or pastor a church

whether you lead a corporation or lead worship.

In his best-selling *Book of Virtues*, William Bennett quips, "There are no menial jobs. Only menial attitudes."

The last weekend of the summer, I honored all the people in our church who work for the public schools—administration, teachers, and staff. Asking them to stand, I prayed for their work, for their students, and for the other people working with them. I put them on notice that their job was a ministry, that God had called them to be role models and appointed them to serve the children and families in our community.

A week later, one of our teachers, watery-eyed with the memory of that brief ministry time, thanked me with passion. A Christian for many years, she had not once had any Christian leader (including myself!) affirm her work in public education as a calling from God. It was revolutionary and liberating for her, she told me.

## BORN AGAIN WORK

There's a curse on work. Jesus came to redeem us from the curse of sin and its consequences. When we become Christians we're born again—and all our attitudes about everything, including our work, are supposed to be born again too. Changing jobs may not be the road to happiness. Maybe it's about changing your heart.

To acquire the best possible attitude in the worst possible job, consider Ephesians 6:5-9: "Servants [the word here is "slave" in the original New Testament Greek], respectfully obey your earthly masters but always with an eye to obeying the *real* master, Christ.

"Don't just do what you have to do to get by, but work heartily, as Christ's servants doing what God wants you to do. And work with a smile on your face, always keeping in mind that no matter who happens to be giving the orders, you're really serving God. Good work will get you good pay from the Master, regardless of whether you are slave or free.

"Masters, it's the same with you. No abuse, please, and no threats. You and your servants are both under the same Master in heaven. He makes no distinction between you and them" (Ephesians 6:5-9, *The Message*).

In one place in the old King James Bible it says that God is "no respecter of persons." In other words, God doesn't care what kind of work you do as much as he cares about how you do what you're doing. Some people are given multiple talents. Some only one. God is not counting what you have, but he's counting on what you do with what you have. God is watching for faithfulness.

When your work is "born again," everything begins to change: "Then I realized," Solomon wrote, "that it is good and proper for a man to eat and drink, and to find satisfaction in his toilsome labor under the sun during the few days of life God has given him—for this is his lot." It's the will of God!

"Moreover, when God gives any man wealth and possessions, and enables him to enjoy them, *to accept his lot and be happy in his work*—this is a gift of God. He seldom reflects on the days of his life, because God keeps him occupied with gladness of heart" (Ecclesiastes 5:18-20).

## MAKING GODLESS WORK GODLY

Rogers and King suggest nine Christian things you can do when your job isn't really Christian:
- Respect those in authority over you.
- Seek to develop mutual respect and trust among your co-workers.
- Seek to relate to others in peace and harmony.
- Do good to others and treat them the way they want to be treated.
- Forgive those who offend you.
- Show mercy towards others.
- Love other people you work with by meeting their needs in tangible, practical ways. Be helpful.
- Purposefully do nice things for people. Even Jesus commands us to do this: "Love your enemies, do good to those who hate you, bless those who curse you, pray for those who mis-

treat you.... If someone takes your cloak, do not stop him from taking your tunic.... If you love those who love you, what credit is that to you? Even 'sinners' love those who love them. And if you do good to those who do good to you, what credit is that to you? Even 'sinners' do that" (Luke 6:27-33).

*   Pray—for yourself, for your work, and for others who work with you.[4]

I was meeting in my office with a woman in our church who teaches through television, radio, and seminars, on finding God's will in a career and God's peace in work. Her ministry has touched over ten thousand people, most of them Christians.

"Not one," she recounted with grief, "Not one has told me that he or she prayed about what kind of work they should do."

---

**AND IN THE NEXT CHAPTER... HOW YOUR**

**MONEY CAN MAKE YOU HAPPY.**

---

## SEVEN

## HOLY MONEY! BATMAN

*How your money can make you happy*

Gato, our cat, drank all the sugar water in our Christmas tree stand. The evergreen isn't. It's crispy dry, almost brown. Another holiday season is history.

Actually, it's New Year's Eve day, and David and Jill, right now your two vehicles are tiny specks inching across the Arizona badlands back to the Pacific Coast.

Yes, *two* vehicles. You moved to California a year ago. And now you had to rent a U-Haul to cart *more* furniture and *more* stuff to your tiny apartment. There you are, Dave, driving alone in the orange-and-white mini-truck, and there you are, Jill, alone in the Geo—for eight grueling hours. Knowing what you had ahead of you made you think about ... *walkie-talkies!*

Yes! That was just what you needed!

You were just minutes from leaving our home when you, Dave, blurted out to Jill, "Why don't we go buy a pair of walkie-talkies?"

"How much? Five dollars?" Jill asked innocently.

*Both* you and I (I felt your heart, Dave) answered nearly at the same time: "No, more like $30 or $40."

"That much!" Jill gasped. "And Dave, we had planned to

leave almost two hours ago," she pleaded. "We don't have time to shop for walkie-talkies!"

Silence.

I could see it on your face, Dave. You were thinking to yourself, "Now that was a stupid idea." It was the tone of her voice, wasn't it, Dave? You knew that was "end of discussion" and you wouldn't be considering walkie-talkies for a long time. Probably not until next Christmas.

It's little things like that. And big ones, like whether to pay off your car or trade it in for one of those smokin' year-end lease deals. It's even bigger ones, like whether to rent a condo or buy a house. It's how much to spend

on clothes,
and music,
and videos,
and furniture,
and electronics,
and computer software,
and dinner out,
and sports equipment,
and vacation,
and … the anxiety and tension of it all.

### IF IT'S ON SALE, YOU NEED IT

Last year, when I spoke to the church about stewardship, I actually talked Mom into doing a "top ten" as a part of my sermon.

How much Mom likes to shop (I didn't say *spend*, did I?) *and* how she *hates* to speak in public are both common knowledge in the church. So when she came up on the platform, the congregation gave her a rousing cheer.

"The Top Ten things I've taught my husband about money," she began.

Number 10: Get it now. Tomorrow it might be gone.

Number  9: If it's on sale, you need it.

Number  8: You can always take it back.

Number  7: So many malls, shops, stores, boutiques, so little time.

Number  6: If you put it on your credit card, it's not really spending money.

Number  5: There's no such thing as compulsive shopping. Just enthusiastic shopping.

Number  4: Shopping is patriotic. It's good for the economy.

Number  3: If you've still got checks, there must be money in the account.

Number  2: If you want it, you deserve it.

**Number  1: As you go from mall to mall, if the shoe fits, buy it!**

Except for Number 8, none of this is true of Mom, but sad to say it's indicative of the way many people really do think about money. Maybe you could call these the "top ten commandments of consumerism."

## STRESSING OVER MONEY

David and Jill, did you know that stress over money is thought to be the number one cause of marriage conflict? Just a couple years ago, Robert Wuthnow published a landmark book, *God and Mammon in America,* based on a five-year study on religious and economic beliefs among a representative sample of more than two thousand members of the U.S. work force.

Among other things, Wuthnow found that 88 percent of those surveyed were bothered a little or a lot that they didn't have enough money, and 72 percent were worried a little or a lot about how they were going to pay their bills. Over 70 percent admitted feeling some or a lot of anxiety over decisions about money, and over half confessed they had some guilt over the things they were spending money for.[1]

Perhaps the most significant finding, at least from my perspective, is that two out of three (including two out of every three people who attend church regularly!) agreed with the statement: *"Money is one thing, morals and values are completely separate."*

David and Jill, this *is* the problem. People just don't get it— that how you manage and spend your money has nothing to do with money and everything to do with life values. Chris Wolfard—you know our business administrator at our church and personal friend for twenty years—says this: *The way you spend your money is your religion.*

If this were not true, if there is no relationship between money and morals, then why do people go ballistic over taxes, or the way the government spends our dollars? Can't you just hear it? "It's *immoral* how the government wastes our hard-earned money!"

Or the way the church wastes its money?

Or the way a spouse spends money, as in, *"I'm* the breadwinner in this family and *I'm* going to decide how the money is spent, *not you."*

Admit it, how you budget your money … or spend it … or squander it … or save and invest it is about what's inside you. The love of money, the Bible claims, is the root of all evil. Like a magic key, money unlocks the secret loves of a person's heart. Money is about power and control, about what's really important to people. That's why money without self-restraint is self-destructive, even addictive, and why it is so utterly necessary to give money away.

## THE MARSHMALLOW PRINCIPLE

Last year, a new book, *Emotional Intelligence,* garnered a cover story in *Time* magazine by Nancy Gibbs. She writes, "a scientist can see the future by watching four-year-olds interact with a marshmallow. The researcher invites the children, one by one, into a plain room and begins the gentle torment. 'You can have this marshmallow right now,' he says. 'But if you wait while I run an errand, you can have two marshmallows when I get back.' And then he leaves."

Some of the "torturees" wolf down the marshmallow within seconds of the door closing. Others wait, cleverly distracting themselves by singing, by trying to look away, or even by falling asleep. When the researcher returns, the patient ones are rewarded. And then, Gibbs reports, "science waits for them to grow up."

What they have discovered is nothing short of remarkable. "A survey of the children's parents and teachers found that those who as four-year-olds had the fortitude to hold out for the second marshmallow generally grew up to be better adjusted, more popular, adventurous, confident, and dependable teenagers.

"The children who gave in to the temptation early on were more likely to be lonely, easily frustrated, and stubborn. They buckled under stress and shied away from challenges. And when some of the students in the two groups took the Scholastic Aptitude Test, the kids who had held out longer scored an average of 210 points higher."[1]

Yale physiologist Peter Salovey and the University of New Hampshire's John Mayer coined a term to describe this behavior: *emotional intelligence,* or EQ. And the new book, *Emotional Intelligence,* by Harvard-trained Daniel Goleman, was written to redefine what it means to be smart. Goleman's thesis: success is based less on IQ than on life skills—*character*. The *Time* article goes on to say that *deficient emotional skills may be the reason more than half of all marriages end in divorce*.

It's a character issue!

It's a matter of the heart.

Even a "secular" book, *Money Doesn't Grow On Trees*, on teaching your children about money, recognizes the emotional power of money: "While the body of literature on parenting deals with a range of subjects, it is odd that no book [*no book!*] addresses one particularly vital skill that a child will use every day of his or her adult life: money management. The reason? The overwhelming majority of Americans—some say as high as 80 percent—don't understand finance themselves. How money works and, more important, how it can work for the person using it is a mystery to many, many otherwise intelligent people....

"Second, *money is an emotionally-charged subject*. It is viewed as 'the root of all evil,' as a tool for power, or as a weapon to control others. Money evokes such strong emotions that it is cited as the number one reason for divorce in the country."[2]

## RISING BANKRUPTCY AND AN
## INCOMPREHENSIBLE NATIONAL DEBT

Meanwhile, American families are enslaved by debt. A recent top-of-the-front-page-article in the Phoenix newspaper warned, "Credit debt spirals toward disaster: counseling service fears 'house of cards' is doomed to collapse." According to Consumer Credit Counseling Service here in Phoenix, personal income has increased 17 percent since 1992, but consumer debt has increased 36 percent.

This year people owe more than ever, over $400 billion, but people just keep borrowing and owing. There are 1 billion credit

cards in the U.S., 5 per adult! And 19 per cent of disposable income goes to paying off consumer debt—paying for interest. In Phoenix alone, the number of bankruptcies increased by a whopping 41 percent in just one year, from 1995 to 1996.

Either you will master your money, or your money will master you. Or to say it another way, either what's inside of you will master your life, or you choose a Master to help control what's inside you.

Money is a lot like sex and work. It's *spiritual.* Yet Robert Wuthnow found that only one in three people in the American workforce gave any thought to the connection between religious values and their personal finances. That means two-thirds of them didn't![3]

If money isn't a spiritual issue, why do our multi-trillion dollar national debt and record levels of personal indebtedness seem to run parallel to our national and personal rejection of God?

Take God out of the workplace, and *curse work.* Your job becomes your god.

Take God out of your sex life, and *curse sex.* Sex for pleasure becomes your god.

Take God out of your checkbook, and *curse your money.* Your wealth becomes your god.

Take God out of your heart, and *curse your heart.* Your greed becomes your god.

You gotta have the marshmallow, and you gotta have it now.

*Money!* It's huge. So you'd better talk openly about it a lot, fully accepting the fact that your differences and personal feelings about money won't just melt away in the heat of your love. Realistically, you will probably never agree entirely on how to manage and spend every dollar, but you can agree to communicate, to take time to think things through, and to ask advice if you get stuck. "Money is no more evil than electricity," write Godfrey and Edwards. "Both have the ability to inflict enormous distress and destruction. It is the user who decides."[4]

David and Jill, personal money management is not my specialty, but I have a smattering of advice that, if you listen, will put your money skills way ahead of most young couples.

*First, set up a family budget.*

Sadly, only 1 in 4 households in America develops and sticks to a family budget, according to a recent study done by Visa, USA. *These people didn't plan to fail ... they failed to plan.*

There's a potent passage in the Bible on this: "At the end of your life you will groan, when your flesh and body are spent. You will say, 'How I hated discipline! How my heart spurned correction! I would not obey my teachers or listen to my instructors. I have come to the brink of ruin'" (Proverbs 5:11-14).

*Yeah, you need a budget.*

A budget is a wise plan that lays out what you will do with your money. A budget enables you to pay for what you need and save up for what you want. According to Godfrey and Edwards, a budget encourages a person of any age to face the consequences of spending money, and to discipline the urge we all have for instant gratification[5]—the marshmallow principle.

## THE BENEFITS OF A PERSONAL BUDGET

My good friend and colleague Bob Blayter, who teaches seminars on financial freedom, came up with a list of budget benefits. I learned them the hard way, Dave and Jill. I discovered, to my distress, that the more money Mom and I made, the less able we were to manage it. It was like, oh, we can pay this off. We can afford that.

Well, next thing I knew we owed nearly $5000 on our VISA credit card and lots of money on other things. Feeling like I was tumbling into the Twilight Zone of consumer debt, I slithered into Bob's office and begged him to tell me about his famous budgeting system.

I did it. *We* did it. It worked, and I am living proof of the "six benefits" of budgeting:

**Budget Benefit #1:** A budget gives you the discipline *not to spend*. A budget doesn't really control your money. It controls you. Or at least it's a guardrail on the winding road of sales and super sales.

Bob Blayter likes to ask his seminar participants, "If you see something on sale, let's say...

## 60% OFF
## ONE DAY ONLY

will you make the purchase even if you don't have the money in your budget?" If you say yes, the best budget in the world won't help you. But if your heart is right ... and you know that two marshmallows later are better than one right now, then yes, a budget will work!

**Budget Benefit #2:** A budget gives you the *freedom to spend*. It's like a $100 bill in a Christmas card. It's *free* money, *spending* money, *mall* money—*fun* money! When have you ever used birthday or Christmas cash to pay a bill?

Conversely, when you don't have a budget, you're never quite sure if you can buy this or afford that. "Afford" is not even a word in your vocabulary. It's more like, "Do we *need* this? Do we *want* this?" And then every purchase is tinged with guilt. Some are soaked in it.

A budget makes shopping fun! You can actually feel good about spending money, because you're mastering it with thoughtfulness and using it with care. It's how your money can make you happy!

**Budget Benefit #3:** A budget will reduce the number of fights you have about money, because a budget forces you both to agree ahead of time how you are going to save and spend your money. It's kind of like the budget becomes bigger than either of you. Leaders in the business world might call this a "vision-driven budget," as opposed to a "personality or personal interest-driven budget."

**Budget Benefit #4:** A budget will enable you to get your bills paid off so you can start saving your money. Remarkably, *hundreds* of families in our church have escaped the prison of debt in twelve to twenty-four months, simply by setting up and sticking to a family budget ... and sacrificing a little now to get out of debt a little later.

Yep, it's the two-for-one-marshmallow again. E.Q.

Some people whine, "But I don't have enough money for a budget. I just don't earn enough to make ends meet, and if I worked out a budget, it would just make me depressed."

Well, now there's a mindless response if I ever heard one. Go ahead then, just keep spending your money without thinking about it. Not thinking about it is going to make all your problems go away. Right? Sooner or later everything will just work out. Right?

Wrong!

This is the ostrich principle (another deep theological concept right up there with the marshmallow principle): Just stick your head in the sand and no one will notice your big, ugly ... um ... well ... *debt!*

*Things will always get worse before they get better until you decide to do the right thing.*

**Budget Benefit #5:** A budget helps with long-range personal financial planning. According to the same Visa USA study I just mentioned, only two out of ten people plan more than a year ahead.

I can vouch for the truth of this one personally, too, because before we had a budget, while I was making more money than ever before, Mom and I did not have a long-term personal financial plan. Know why? It was all we could do to keep up our credit payments and try to get our short-term loans paid down. But, *hear me on this*, we could not get our short-term debt paid down because we kept buying things without knowing if we could really afford them. And we didn't know if we could afford them, because we didn't have a budget. *It was a vicious circle.*

Budgeting our expenses, though, enabled us to break the cycle of credit and more credit, and for the first time ever, within less than two years after developing our family budget, we had a long term financial plan.

**Budget Benefit #6:** A budget helps keep your checkbook balanced. This may seem like a small bonus, but my budget has dramatically improved my ability to keep an accurate checkbook ledger. How? It's simple math. Two accounting systems are better than one. I'll show you how.

On pages 125-26 is a simple family budget planner to get you started. If you need personal help, call your local bank. They should have people to assist you with your personal finances. If they don't, change banks!

*Second, save as much as you can.*

Remember, I was giving you a few bits of basic advice. More than anything else, you need a budget. Second, you need to save, for lots of good reasons....

- Money in the bank gives you flexibility and peace of mind.

- It's always better to pay cash. When you save up to pay for something you need or want, *you* get the compounded interest, not the bank or the credit card company. When you save, it's like you're making payments to yourself.

- Financial planners say it's important to save up the equivalent of about six months of your personal income to protect yourself against job loss or illness.

There are a couple of pretty good Bible verses about saving your money, too:

"Dishonest money dwindles away, but he who gathers money little by little makes it grow" (Proverbs 13:11).

# FAMILY BUDGET GUIDE

| INCOME PER MONTH | TOTAL |
|---|---|
| GROSS INCOME:<br>  Salary _____    Interest _____<br>  Dividends _____    Other _____ | |
| LESS:   Tithe _____<br>          Tax (est./Fed., State, FICA) _____ | |
| (#1) Net Spendable Income: | |

| EXPENSES | TOTAL |
|---|---|
| HOUSING:<br>  Mortgage/Rent _____    Electric _____<br>  Insurance _____    Gas _____<br>  Taxes _____    Water _____<br>  Maintenance _____    Sanitation _____<br>  Other _____    Telephone _____ | |
| FOOD: | |
| AUTOMOBILE:<br>  Payment _____    Insurance _____<br>  Gas/Oil _____    Tags/Taxes _____<br>  Maintenance/Repairs/Replacement _____ | |
| INSURANCE:    Life _____<br>  Medical _____    Other _____ | |
| DEBTS:<br>  Credit Cards _____    Loan/Note _____<br>  Other _____    Other _____ | |

| | |
|---|---|
| **ENTERTAINMENT/RECREATION:**<br>    Eating Out   _____    Vacation   _____<br>    Baby Sitting   _____    Activities   _____<br>    Other   _____    Trips   _____ | |
| **CLOTHING:** | |
| **SAVINGS:** | |
| **MEDICAL EXPENSES:**<br>    Doctor   _____    Drugs   _____<br>    Dentist   _____    Other   _____ | |
| **MISCELLANEOUS:**<br>    Toiletry/Cosmetics _____ Beauty/Barber_____<br>    Laundry/Cleaning _____ Subscriptions _____<br>    Allowances/Lunch _____ Cash _____<br>    Gifts (Include Christmas) _____ Other _____ | |
| **SCHOOL/CHILD CARE:**<br>    Transportation _____    Tuition _____<br>    Day Care _____    Materials _____ | |
| **INVESTMENTS:** | |
| (#2) Total Expenses: | |

## SUMMARY: INCOME VS. EXPENSES

Net Spendable Income:.....................................(#1)   _____

LESS: Expenses:.................................................(#2)   _____

Unallocated Surplus Income ...........................(#3)   _____

"In the house of the wise are stores of choice food and oil, but a foolish man devours all he has" (Proverbs 21:20). In other words, a fool is driven by his need for immediate gratification!

*Third, give away as much as you can, at least 10 percent.*

There's a secret to staying faithful to your budget. It's this: *Turn the ownership of your money over to God, because when God's in control, you're in control.* Make Jesus the Lord of your checkbook.

Solomon wrote, "Honor the Lord with your wealth, with the firstfruits of all your crops; then your barns will be filled to overflowing, and your vats will brim over with new wine" (Proverbs 3:9-10).

The myth is that God wants to take everything away from you because he knows that you will never be truly happy unless you have nothing. And the church's business is to get you to give, give, give until they have all your money, or until you are finally broken of every vestige of selfishness, or both. Probably both.

The reality is that money is a medium of exchange. It's part of life. God wants you to acknowledge that everything you have ultimately belongs to him and that budgeting and being generous with what you have keeps the power of money in check. When you release the control of your money to God, manage your resources carefully as if they didn't belong to you (they belong to God, Jesus is Lord), and decide to be a generous person, *your money will make you happy.*

And you will be unhappy and your misery index will rise to the degree you don't do these things. Listen to Jesus. It's a no-brainer: "It is more blessed to give than to receive" (Acts 20:35). Giving is always better for you than getting.

OK, so let's assume that the church is always asking for money—and that it wastes every dime you give. In my humble opinion, when people talk about how they don't like to give to church, for whatever reason, it's just a lame excuse, because it's very likely they are not giving their money anywhere.

Actually, my humble opinion is corroborated by a Lily Endowment Fund study in 1995 which found that church members are giving a smaller portion of their income to churches, but are going into debt to purchase more luxury items. The study also found that church funding for overseas missions has been flat since 1987, at about $2 billion. In comparison, Americans spend $4 billion a year on crafts, $32 billion on diet programs, and $40 billion on leisure travel.[6]

Well, tell me then, why are we so unhappy? Because it is less blessed to receive than to give. I love the headline over a little article in the local paper: "Doctor prescribes giving to mend societal ill." The article quoted physician Clifford Harris, a long-time contributor to the United Way who said, "It's part of our responsibility in life. We should all tithe. We should give back to society without even being asked, really. You can't just take all the time. You've got to give back."

*Tithing in the newspaper!* What's the world coming to?

## TITHING? WHAT'S THAT?

Generally, tithing is giving *regularly* and *proportionately*: "On the first day of every week, each one of you should set aside a sum of money in keeping with his income, saving it up, so that when I come no collections will have to be made" (1 Corinthians 16:2).

Tithing, simply, is a way to budget your giving. More specifically, tithing is giving 10 percent of your income (I suggest your *gross* income), preferably to a local church. If for some reason it rankles you to give to a church, give anywhere. Just give. I dare ya.

Like budgeting, tithing has multiple benefits. *First*, it brings order into the chaos of your personal finances. If you think you are having a hard time making ends meet and you are not tithing, believe me, tithing will force you to seriously rethink the way you manage your personal finances.

*Tithing is God's way to get me to live on 90 percent of my income, so that what I have is always enough. Credit cards and unmanaged debt are the devil's way to get me to live on 110 percent of my income, so that what I have is never enough.*

You can't afford to tithe? Listen, you can't afford not to tithe! I have *never* had someone who tithes tell me he can't afford it, or that he regrets it, or that it has created financial hardship. On the other hand, I've heard lots of people howling like alley cats about tithing *before* they try it, because of unrealistic fears.

Which leads me to the *second* benefit of tithing: spiritual growth. Tithing is not, ultimately, about money. It's not even about supporting the church. It's about your heart. God doesn't want your money; he wants what it represents.

I think one of the most profound things I ever read about money is a statement by Christian writer Jacques Ellul in his book *Money and Power:* "We should meditate on this fact and think of it each Sunday at the time of the offering. The offering is not a utilitarian act, and we should stop thinking of it that way, that this is the way to support the church. *The offering, the moment of giving, should be for us the moment when we renounce the power of mammon and the world and show our dedication to the Lord.*"[7]

*Third,* believe it or not, tithing could virtually wipe out world hunger. I read recently that if church members were to boost their giving to an average of 10 percent of their income, the additional funds could eliminate the worst of world poverty, which James Grant, the executive director of UNICEF, says would require $65 billion. The 10 percent would provide that *plus* another $17 billion for domestic need—all the while maintaining church activities at current levels.

*Fourth*, tithing is a key to unlimited blessing. It puts God on your side in a major way. God is speaking in Malachi 3:8-12: "'Will a man *rob* God? Yet you rob me. But you ask, "How do we rob you?" *In tithes and offerings. You are under a curse*—the whole nation of you [everyone is affected]—because you are robbing me. Bring the *whole* tithe into the storehouse [the local church?], that there may be food [good sermons and good ministry] in my house.

"'*Test me in this*,' says the Lord Almighty, 'and see if I will not throw open the floodgates of heaven and pour out so much blessing that you will not have room enough for it. I will prevent pests [taxes, inflation, and a failing social security system] from devouring your crops [ruining your future], and the vines in your fields will not drop their fruit,' says the Lord Almighty. 'Then all the nations will call you blessed [they will want to know your secret, but they won't believe you when you tell them that you're tithing], for yours will be a delightful land,' says the Lord Almighty."

We are so convinced that God means what he says, our church offers people a ninety-day, money-back guarantee if they'll give tithing a chance.

It works.

Someone sent this anonymous letter to me. It's not really about tithing, but it is a wonderful example of someone who understands God's ownership of our resources:

Enclosed is my first paycheck, the firstfruits from my new job. This job was granted to me by my Lord Jesus. It was won by and through the prayers of many people and ultimately by the grace of God. I praise and thank God every day for this and many other blessings. I promised Jesus my first financial fruits when hired and even though this job brings me great joy and hope, the highlight of my new employment is the privilege of giving back. Thank you Jesus.

I pray for you, David and Jill, and for all the other young couples reading this book, that the highlight of your earning power will be the privilege of giving a portion of what you earn back to God.

Well, so much for my smattering of advice. If you need more thorough information, I suggest you search a local Christian bookstore or even the Internet. Check out Larry Burkett's Website at www.cfcministry.org. As I already mentioned, even your local bank should have financial counseling available. They'll give you a major credit card at the drop of a hat, and so you should expect them to help you manage your money so you can make your payments and keep your good credit.

---

**AND IN THE NEXT CHAPTER, HOW TO MAKE**

**SURE YOUR MARRIAGE LASTS A LIFETIME....**

---

---

## EIGHT

## SUPERGLUE

---

*Putting God first*

A cabin full of sixth-grade boys.

And me.

For two nights in October, Dave was one of the enemy.

(Did Dave ever tell you this story, Jill?)

When I volunteered to be a counselor at Dave's class camp, they didn't tell me I'd have to do it alone.

Trying to be your pals' big buddy and best friend, Dave, was a terrible mistake. When an innocent pillow fight turned ugly, I lost it. Deep inside I had this awful feeling that someone was going to die, and I told myself it wasn't going to be me.

Surrounded by three walls of bunks filled with twelve-year-olds hurling lethal objects, I stood up on my rickety camp bed in the middle of the maelstrom, put on my worst face, and started yelling at the top of my lungs. I threatened you little monsters with your very lives.

It was like the fear of God. Well, maybe it was more like a perversion of the fear of God. Do you remember that you were too frightened to get out of bed to go to the toilet?

To this day I'm grateful that those boys didn't know your

father was a pastor, because that night I acted more like the devil than a man of God.

But it worked. The dark silence was awesome, and within minutes everyone was asleep.

### WHATEVER

I don't know how he does it, but your Uncle Dave teaches seventh graders every day all day nine months a year. Not too long ago he was telling me how so many of his students are terribly disrespectful. Often, when he has to correct them in front of their friends, and they really don't want to bend under his authority, their last gasp of defiance is the way cool word, "What*EVER*." Like, "Teacher, I hear you, but I'm not going to give you the satisfaction that I agree. Not at all."

Uncle Dave has given that some deep thought. He's making banners for other teachers in the school for their classrooms. Banners that announce:

*What EVER* means ... *teacher wins.*

I don't think you've seen it, Dave, but above the new entry gate at your old elementary school they posted the sign, "We believe in respect." You know why they have to do that? Because people disrespect one another with a passion. That's one of the reasons why we moved your little brother Matt to another school. There was chaos in his classroom, and his teacher, a good and dedicated man, seemed powerless to make a difference.

You're a researcher now, Dave. A pollster of sorts. So I don't really have to tell you about statistics, about how multiple studies have shown that the breakup of the family is the principal cause of our insurmountable social problems. Yet when politicians talk about values, their rhetoric is anchorless because of something far more sinister: *godlessness.* We don't really have a moral crisis in America. At least that's not the heart of the problem. Our real problem is a crisis of godlessness.

## GODLESS CHRISTIAN HOMES

Now by "godless" I don't mean the worst imaginable wickedness, although godlessness and wickedness certainly go hand in hand. I do mean "godless," though, in the sense that God is a non-factor in our public institutions and in so many of our homes. Even Christian families can be godless. You can say you believe in Jesus, and you can go to church faithfully, all the while living your life like everybody else around you. As if there really were no God.

> Oh, the joys of those
> who do not follow the advice of the wicked,
> or stand around with sinners
> or join in with scoffers.
> But they delight in doing everything the Lord wants;
> day and night they think about his law.
>
> PSALM 1:1-2, *The New Living Bible*

In the old King James Version of the Bible, the first verse says, "Blessed is the man that walketh not in the *counsel of the ungodly.*" People who are ungodly make their decisions and live their lives as though there is no God. In fact, that's how the Bible defines "fool": "The fool has said in his heart, 'There is no God'" (Psalm 14:1, *New King James Version*).

According to the Bible, a fool is not someone who's an idiot. It's not even someone who has philosophical questions about the existence of God. The Bible is not spouting off, "An atheist is a fool." Instead, God's Word points us to the effects of a life without God. And what's that like? According to Psalm 14:1-3:

They are corrupt, their deeds are vile;
>   there is no one who does good.
The Lord looks down from heaven on the sons of men
>   to see if there are any who understand,
>   any who seek God.
All have turned aside,
>   they have together become corrupt;
there is no one who does good, not even one.

"Godless" is family, work, and leisure without God. Without acknowledging God's laws. Without an anchor. The opposite is "God-fearing." We never actually used this term around the house. It sounds kind of old-fashioned, but it's what people used to call other people when they did noble and responsible things, as in, "Them people are sure *God-fearin'* folk."

I have this simple conviction that God-fearing people were the main reason why life used to be more ordered, and people used to respect one another more, and kids in the public schools used to be less hostile, and divorce was something that hardly ever happened. But...

Hear the word of the Lord...
>   because the Lord has a charge to bring
>   against you who live in the land:
"There is no faithfulness, no love,
>   [Why??? Because there is]
>   *no acknowledgment of God in the land.*
>   [So instead and because of that]
There is only cursing, lying and murder,
>   stealing and adultery;
they break all bounds,
>   and bloodshed follows bloodshed.          HOSEA 4:1-2

Sounds just like America, doesn't it? Godless, not God-fearing—adrift in a sea of sin, violence, and broken lives. In sharp contrast, the fear of the Lord is a definition of true religion in the Old Testament and is what causes people to obey God's commandments.

One of the greatest passages in the Old Testament affirms this: "These are the commands, decrees and laws the Lord your God directed me to teach you to observe ... so that you, your children and their children after them *may fear the Lord your God* as long as you live [How?] by keeping all his decrees and commands that I give you, and so that you may enjoy long life. Hear, O Israel, and be careful to obey so that it may go well with you and that you may increase greatly"(Deuteronomy 6:1-3).

Not too long ago I was studying the book of Proverbs, and one of my commentaries said that "the fear of the Lord" refers both to the sense of awe human beings feel in the presence of God *and to the respect they show towards the Lord's intentions and teaching.*[1] When you fear someone in a healthy way, you respect them. And when you respect them, you respect what they have to say.

## MEEK AND SUBMISSIVE HUSBANDS

So, what's it all to you, Dave and Jill?

Ephesians 5 is the most quoted chapter in the Bible on the subject of the Christian home. In verse 25, Paul commands you, David, to love Jill as much as and in the same way that Jesus loves his bride the church.

And Jill, verse 22 is just a little controversial: "Wives submit to your husbands as to the Lord ... in *everything*." I'm your father-in-law, so I won't press that one.

Actually, the secret to a happy marriage is not a meek and fully submissive wife! It's *two* people who are fully submissive to one another. That's how Paul gets himself into the submission debate in the first place. Before he says a word about wives submitting to their husbands and husbands loving their wives, he lays out the overriding principle: "Submit to one another out of reverence for Christ"(Ephesians 5:21).

The meaning of this verse is clear, but here are a couple of other translations to make it more obvious: "Out of respect for Christ, be courteously reverent to one another" (*The Message*). "And fit in with each other, because of your common reverence for Christ" (J. B. Phillips).

Sorry, but I can't remember if I spoke about this verse at your wedding last December. I wanted to say something original, because I've used Ephesians 5:21 at nearly every other wedding I've done: "Submit to one another out of reverence to Christ." I've told couple after couple that this verse is the SuperGlue of marriage for two reasons. First, because it's about giving in.

### BUT... BUT... BUTT

Just last night your brother Matt and I were watching a Discovery Channel program about Australian wild dogs. Dingoes. One segment showed two of the animals with their teeth locked on either end of the remains of a poor rabbit they were having for dinner. In not much time at all, what was left of the rabbit was in two more ragged pieces.

It was a sickening scene that made me think about people. Teeth clenched. Snarling. Refusing to let go of their end of a dead rabbit.

"Submit to one another," the Bible says.

While I'm thinking about animal stories, I heard one time of a particular kind of mountain goat. When two of these high country hardheads confront one another on a single-lane precipice, after some time of head-butting and cold-eyed staring, one of the two goats will actually lie down on the narrow path, allowing the other to walk over his fully submitted body. That way, in the end, both goats get what they want.

"Submit to one another…."

But… But… Butt.

But how?

In reality, two people by sheer will power can't just stop butting one another. David, you should know. You've seen Mom and me sinking deep in the quicksand of misunderstanding, anger, and pain.

It's so hard just to lie down and take it. To give in. To give up. What you and Jill fight about will always seem so important to both of you. Even when no one else in the world would think it was important.

How do you break the cycle?

That's the second part of Ephesians 5:21: "Submit to one another *out of reverence for Christ.*" A good marriage is not just about trying hard to love each other, which is impossible at times. It's about making Jesus Lord of your marriage, your thoughts, and your emotions. You *must* do this. There is no reasonable alternative.

This is where we come back to the fear of God. Remember what I wrote earlier? The reason why we have so many problems in our world is because people are not *God-fearing.* When nations lose their moral conscience, they are like great rudderless ships, and nations and people lose their conscience when they lose their fear of God.

Marriage is the best example of all. "Submit to one another." But … Can't do that. Won't do that. Ever. "Submit to one another!" But how? *"… out of reverence for Christ."* When you share "reverence for Christ," you're not only into something bigger than the both of you, but you're also inviting the Lord Jesus into your conflict and pain, to heal you and to enable you to do what you can't do in your own strength.

## GODLESS STAINED GLASS

The Greek word translated "reverence" is *phobos*, which simply means "fear." "Reverence" is softer, more user-friendly than F—E—A—R. For some people, reverence is a good religious feeling when they're holding their baby in church, and soft, colored light is shining, just right, through the stained glass windows.

Now you know that both your mom and I, raised Lutheran,

have a genuine appreciation for stained glass—and the great church traditions it represents. But the "fear of the Lord" is so much more. The fear of God is a deep conviction that when you violate his laws, there is a terrible price to pay.

Years ago, people referred to marriage as "*holy* matrimony." Matrimony isn't holy if you don't acknowledge God as the Maker and Sustainer of your marriage. You probably didn't know that the old, traditional wedding ceremony, in the event that the bride and groom are just doing it for romantic reasons, solemnly reminds the wedding party and the congregation that we are all standing before God. Just ahead in life is "that dreadful day of judgment."

What an unlovely thought at a lovely wedding! Why should we think about things like that when the room is filled with flowers and lace. And the light through the stained glass is just right.

But it *is* a dreadful thing to fall into the hands of an angry God. It's even worse, much worse, than your dad in a rage in a cabin at your class camp. Even the New Testament, where we read all about God's love and grace and forgiveness, gets edgy about this.

"So don't turn a deaf ear to these gracious words," the writer of Hebrews warns us. "If those who ignored earthly warnings didn't get away with it, what will happen to us if we turn our backs on heavenly warnings? His voice that time [at Mount Sinai, when he gave the Ten Commandments] shook the earth to its foundations; this time—he's told us this quite plainly— he'll also rock the heavens...

"Do you see what we've got? An unshakable kingdom! And do you see how thankful we must be? Not only thankful, but brimming with worship, *deeply reverent before God*. For God is not an indifferent bystander. He's actively cleaning house, torching all that needs to burn, and he won't quit until it's all cleansed. God himself is Fire!" (Hebrews 12:25-29, *The Message*)

Proverbs 9:10 puts it this way: "The *fear of the Lord* is the beginning of wisdom." A couple of years ago around Father's Day, *USA Today* ran a special article about African-American families. I can't forget the advice one father gave his family. There are only three rules you need to know, he announced. First, put God first. Second, put God first. Third, put God first.

When you put God first, you will submit to one another— *out of reverence for Christ*, because "those who *fear the Lord* are secure; he will be a place of refuge for their children" (Proverbs 14:26, *The New Living Bible*).

And Dave and Jill, "Do not let your heart envy sinners, but always be zealous for *the fear of the Lord*. There is surely a future hope for you, and your hope will not be cut off" (Proverbs 23:17-18).

"My son [and daughter-in-law!]... Trust in the Lord with all your heart and lean not on your own understanding; in all your ways acknowledge him, and he will make your paths straight" (Proverbs 3:1, 5-6).

David and Jill, put God first.

---

**AND IN THE NEXT CHAPTER... HOW TO PUT GOD FIRST, HOW TO BE AS GODLY AS YOU CAN BE WITHOUT PUTTING EACH OTHER OFF, WITHOUT BEING OBNOXIOUS.**

---

---

## NINE

## HOW TO BE GODLY WITHOUT
## BEING OBNOXIOUS

---

*Building a grace-based home*

You're on your way to Phoenix, Dave. Right now. In the air somewhere over the desert. The Chicago Bulls are playing the Suns tonight and we have tickets to the game!

And Jill, you have freedom! For the first time in a year, Dave's not going to be drooling on you.

And Dave, you probably wouldn't take a day off work and fly to Arizona just to see your mom and dad. Well, maybe you would! But to watch the Suns play the World Champion Bulls? That could be an incentive.

I had breakfast this morning with our friend Todd, and you came up in the conversation. Or more accurately, our whole family came up in the conversation.

You know how stressful the ministry can be for us. Lots of vocal people in the church, many of them armchair pastors. That's why Todd was talking about our family, and how he comes to my defense. "Just look at his kids!" he objects. "What does that tell you about Gary's walk with God?"

Isn't it great to have friends like that!

Whatever else people in the church whine about, they are certain to be silenced by the integrity and strength of our home.

Do you remember your remarks, Dave, at our twenty-fifth wedding anniversary event at the church? You made us both cry when you spoke of the *spiritual* impact we have made on you kids. (Sorry, Jill, I know you don't like me calling you "kids!") You especially emphasized how real we have always been with each other. No pretenses. No spiritual charades.

## GRACE MEANS SPACE

Not a few people have asked us how we did it. I've told them flatly, "I'm not entirely sure!" We're not even close to perfect. You both know that's true! But I do think I can identify a couple of key elements of our family's spiritual success. First, above everything else, we have fully recognized the grace and favor of God carrying us along on the stream of our lives.

When I refer to God's grace, I'm thinking about his empowering presence, but when I think of grace, I also think of space. Because we so firmly believe that God in his grace has given each of us space, we have come to believe that to do any less for each other would be downright sinful. Getting rid of sin has never been our mission. Getting and giving grace has always been our passion.

Second, because we're sinners saved by grace and kept by grace, our family has always had a revulsion for self-righteousness—and the judgmental spirituality that comes with it. Yes, every home needs rules, but families *must be* grace-based, not rule-based.

I love the way Eugene Peterson has paraphrased Galatians 3:1-3: "You crazy Galatians! Did someone put a hex on you? Have you taken leave of your senses? Something crazy has happened, for it's obvious that you no longer have the crucified Jesus in clear focus in your lives. His sacrifice on the Cross was certainly set before you clearly enough."

He continues, "Let me put this question to you: How did

your new life begin? Was it by working your heads off to please God? Or was it by responding to God's message to you? Are you going to continue this craziness? For only crazy people would think they could complete by their own efforts what was begun by God. If you weren't smart enough or strong enough to begin it, how do you suppose you could perfect it?" (*The Message*)

This is perhaps one of the most difficult challenges of the Christian life: how to become more spiritual without becoming piously proud and intolerant. Or, how to *be* spiritual without *acting* spiritual. Or simply, *how to put God first without putting off your family and friends.*

## PRETENDING TO BE SPIRITUAL

Years ago Christian author Fritz Ridenour wrote a best-selling book about Paul's letter to the Romans. He titled it *How to Be a Christian without Being Religious.* By "religious" he meant obnoxious spirituality, something many people today refer to less kindly as "toxic religion."

You see, you can fool your friends at church, but you will never fool each other or your children, who will come along someday. Hypocrisy in the family lasts like a stick of butter in a microwave. How often you attend church or how often you read your Bible and pray, matters little if you aren't real with each other.

Yes, pretending is like smog. It's pollution in the fresh air. It's environmental poison and it makes you sick. It will only be when you stop the hypocrisy that you will be able to see past the pretense.

God is real. Heaven and earth are real. So get real. Like Jesus. Spirituality is not about acting out some preconceived idea of what you're supposed to look like if you're a Christian. *Spirituality is about being as much like Jesus as you can be.*

And what I know of Jesus, there was nothing, ever, about his relationship with God that made others feel uncomfortable. Or threatened. Except the Pharisees, whose very name has become a byword for holier-than-thou religion. Jesus had an *attractive* spirituality. He made people feel at ease around him—even though he was the Son of God!

Dave and Jill, do you remember hearing me talk about the very first meeting between Jesus and his disciples? How down-to-earth he was? In the very first chapter of his gospel, John writes, "The next day John [the Baptist] was back at his post with two disciples, who were watching. He looked up, saw Jesus walking nearby, and said, 'Here he is, God's Passover Lamb.'

"The two disciples heard him, and went after Jesus. Jesus looked over his shoulder and said to them, 'What are you after?'

"They said, 'Rabbi' (which means "Teacher"), 'where are you staying?'

"He replied, 'Come along and see for yourself.'

"They came, saw where he was living, and ended up staying with him for the day. It was late afternoon when this happened" (John 1:35-39, *The Message*).

The very first question the disciples asked Jesus was *not* theological! "Where are you staying?" they queried. You should understand this, Dave. People are always curious about where the pastor lives, because they really want to know *how* he lives. Jesus, though, wasn't even slightly annoyed by their "unspiritual" curiosity, and he had nothing to hide. "Come and see for yourself," he replied warmly.

Is that down-to-earth or what? By the way, "down-to-earth" is a less theological way to say "incarnation." God has come down-to-earth to us, where we are, on our level, instead of expecting us to come up to him, where he is, on his level. And he's done it with unconditional love, acceptance, and forgiveness.

## WHERE THE MAN OF GOD GOES TO
## THE BATHROOM

Dave, you know what it's like to live in a pastor's home, to live under the spotlight of unrealistic and, at times, weird expectations. There was the time, for example, when a young man from our church, bumping into me in a baseball card shop, blurted out, "So this is where our tithe money goes." He was "just kidding," of course.

Another time, I remember reading in *Leadership* magazine about a young pastor and his wife who were not able to have children of their own. So they adopted. I know this sounds like a joke, but really, an older woman in his church told him privately that it was really much better when pastors and their wives had children that way.

And just today we had a guest from the church in our home. She's been a friend for years, but when Mom showed her around our new house and into our master bedroom suite, she remarked, with a good deal of laughter of course, "So this is where the man of God goes to the bathroom!"

The very fact that she thought about this betrays how people think about the ministry! You know, Dave, people have complimented me for "being so human." (Like putting the bathroom story in a Christian book?) I've always answered incredulously, "I don't have a clue what else to be!"

People make unrealistic and stupid assumptions about men and women of God. Fact is, Christian families end up putting unrealistic expectations on one another, even when no one in the family is a minister!

God is down-to-earth. God became human in the person of his Son, and by this extraordinary act has avowed the supreme value of our humanity. Jesus did not come to deliver us from our humanity, but to set our humanity free from the curse and consequences of sin.

So I've come to the conclusion that to be fully human, I have to be *down-to-earth*. God expects this from me—no more, no less. If Jesus was spiritual, and Jesus was down-to-earth, then I think it's logical to conclude that "spiritual" and "down-to-earth" are mutually inclusive terms. That's a fancy way to say they go together like Michael Jordan and a basketball. Conversely, someone who claims to be spiritual, but who is not down-to-earth, isn't spiritual.

The apostle Paul, for example, acknowledges a direct correlation between spirituality and the down-to-earth art of conflict resolution. "Brothers [you can include sisters]," he writes, "I could not address you as *spiritual* [there's that word!], but as worldly [the old King James uses the word "carnal"]—mere infants in Christ." Sounds like Paul's calling them a bunch of babies!

"I gave you milk," he complains, "not solid food, for you were not yet ready for it. Indeed, you are still not ready. You are still worldly. For since there is jealousy and quarreling among you, are you not worldly?" (1 Corinthians 3:1-3) In other words, you're spiritual when you're getting along with each other by understanding and valuing your differences. And when you're not, you're not spiritual.

## RELIGION THAT DRIVES YOU TO DRINK

Quoting Bible verses at one another draws the lines of battle. Makes war, not peace. Dave, I bet you can count on one hand the times when I used the Bible to get Mom or you kids to do something. We talked a lot about the laws of God in our home—and how serving Jesus means living out your life in obedience to God's Word. But because I have always had such an aversion for using our spirituality to control others, I could never bring myself to wave the Bible to win a family argument.

I've waved my arms. And I've shouted. But I never dragged God into it, and I'm sure he's grateful.

Beating each other with the Bible is a shameful kind of Christianity, literally, because people end up shamed. You kids were afraid of me at times, and I'm sure I made you ashamed, but I never made you feel like God was on my side. I *never* threatened you with the judgment of God.

David and Jill, don't fool yourself into thinking that God is on one side of a marriage dispute and not on the other. *God is on the side of marriage*, which means that your marriage is bigger than either of you. I heard someone say one time that marriage is like a canoe. A canoe is not a good place to have a fight. It takes a millisecond to realize that the canoe is more important than whatever you're fighting about. God is on the side of the canoe.

Quoting the Bible while looking down your nose is a lot different from learning God's ways together. We're back to the grace thing. Rules put the squeeze on people. Grace is about space. The more grace, the more space. The irony of this is that we think too much grace can lead to anarchy—in our personal lives and in our relationships. The truth of the matter is that rules change nothing. They only tell us what needs to change, while grace changes everything.

A fascinating article recently headlined the front page of *The APA Monitor*, the newspaper of the American Psychological Association. Titled "Psychologists' Faith in Religion Grows," the report noted that "psychologists have traditionally had little faith in the importance of religion in mental health. That may be changing. Research suggests that religious faith may actually enhance mental health."

Perhaps more significantly, the article underscores the extraordinary importance of grace-based religion. "When you look more closely, you find there are certain types of religious expression that seem to be helpful and certain types that seem to be harmful," noted Kenneth Pargament, Ph.D., a psychology professor at Ohio's Bowling Green State University.

"In several studies involving hundreds of subjects, Pargament has found that people who embrace what could be called 'the-sinners-in-the-hands-of-an-angry-God' model do indeed have poorer mental health outcomes. People who feel angry toward God, believe they are being punished for their sins or perceive a lack of emotional support from the church or synagogue typically suffer more distress, anxiety, and depression.

"In stark contrast are people who embrace the 'loving God' model. These people see God as a partner who works with them to resolve problems. They view more difficult situations as opportunities for spiritual growth.... The result? They enjoy more positive mental health outcomes.... Mental health outcomes depend on the way people view their relationship with God."[1]

Furthermore, Richard Gorsuch, Ph.D., of Fuller Theological Seminary's Graduate School of Psychology in Pasadena, California, has examined the correlation between religion and substance abuse. The link between religiousness and non-abuse holds true only if one's religion is "caring and supportive," Gorsuch says.

A "harsh and condemning" religion may actually encourage substance abuse, Gorsuch discovered. In one case study he reviewed, an alcoholic drank to escape a God she felt was cursing her.[2]

So grace is space—and more. Grace isn't just letting people do whatever they want. Quite the opposite. God's grace is life changing energy, the empowerment of the Holy Spirit to do God's will, something I'm helpless to do in my own effort. I am changed, not by *external* pressure to be a better person, but by the power of his Spirit working in me.

I need help inside and out, as Paul writes, "Continue to work out your salvation with fear and trembling, for it is God who works in you *to will and to act* according to his good purpose" (Philippians 2:12-13). I especially like the way Eugene Peterson paraphrases this: "Be energetic in your life of salvation, reverent and sensitive before God. That energy is *God's* energy, an energy deep within you, God himself willing and working at what will give him the most pleasure" *(The Message)*.

## TWELVE INCHES OR TWELVE MILES

Just last weekend, best-selling Christian author Steve Sjogren spoke at our church. He said something I'll never forget: "It's only about twelve inches from your heart to your head, but it's twelve miles from your head to your heart." Rules are a head thing. Grace is a heart thing. It's only about twelve inches from grace to rules, because grace changes everything. But it's about twelve miles from rules to grace, because without God's grace nothing changes.

In no uncertain terms, Jesus declared (maybe he was shouting), "You're hopeless, you religion scholars and Pharisees! Frauds! You keep meticulous account books, tithing on every nickel and dime you get, but on the meat of God's Law, things like fairness and compassion and commitment—the absolute basics!—you carelessly take it or leave it. Careful bookkeeping is commendable, but the basics are required. Do you have any idea how silly you look, writing a life story that's wrong from start to finish, nitpicking over commas and semicolons? *You are blind leaders, for you filter out a mosquito yet swallow a camel"* (Matthew 23:23-24, *The Message*/J. B. Phillips[3]).

I love it! Can you imagine that! Someone trying to swallow a camel? That would kill you quicker than smoking one! Hey, I know that cigarette smoking is terribly damaging to your health, but Dave and Jill, it's pretty clear what Jesus is telling us here, that godly people, for all the right reasons, can get hung up on all the wrong little things.

You just graduated from Biola University, Dave, and I know

how much the Christian faculty and environment there meant to you. I'm sure you'll always remember fondly your years there as four of the most memorable of your life.

Thank God for places like that! For institutions governed by the principles of God's Word! For colleges that require chapel services several times a week! But we've both talked about the down side of "the rules." When your mother and I were students there in the early seventies, we were required to sign off on the big five: no drinking, no dancing, no card playing, no motion pictures, and, for heaven's sake, no smoking!

Then in our last year, because of the national crisis over two new issues, drugs and the war in Vietnam, we had to swear in writing we wouldn't mess with hallucinogenic substances or incite campus rioting. True story.

But how times have changed! Now Biola University has shortened its list of rules and has recommitted itself to what Jesus called, "the more important matters of the law." The Apostle Paul wrote about this too:

> Why not say—as we are being slanderously reported as saying and as some claim that we say—"Let us do evil that good may result" [This is often what people seem to think I'm saying too, when I talk about the unconditional grace of God.]....
>
> Therefore no one will be declared righteous in [God's] sight by observing the law; rather through the law we become conscious of sin....
>
> Through Christ Jesus the law of the Spirit of life sets me free from the law of sin and death. For what the law was powerless to do in that it was weakened by the sinful nature, God did by sending his own Son in the likeness of sinful man to be a sin offering. And so he condemned sin in sinful man in

order that the righteous requirements of the law might be fully met in us, we do not live according the sinful nature [trying our best to obey the rules and failing consistently and miserably], but according to the Spirit.

ROMANS 3:8, 20 AND 8:2-4

## GRACE-BASED HOMES

You know, our church is called "Word of Grace," because the amazing grace of God has been my life message. Grace is more than just a basic Christian doctrine. It's about how you relate to God and how, in turn, you relate to one another.

If your understanding of God is grace-based, then your understanding of love and friendship with others will be grace-based too. And, yes, if your understanding of God is rule-based, then your relationship with each other will also be rule-based.

Even the Ten Commandments are grace-based! Did you know that? The first three commandments are about relationship with God. The third, "keep the Sabbath," was intended to keep us remembering that everything in the created order (the first six days of creation) interfaces with God (the seventh day). The rest of the commandments, then, are about relationship with other people.

So Jesus said, summing up the Ten Commandments, "Love the Lord your God with all your heart and with all your soul and with all your mind. This is the first and greatest commandment. And the second is like it: Love your neighbor as yourself. All the Law and the Prophets hang on these two commandments" (Matthew 22:37-40).

What you think about God and how you relate to him, will determine how you relate to each other. Here's another Bible verse that makes this pretty clear: "Be kind and compassionate to one another, forgiving each other, *just as in Christ God forgave you*" (Ephesians 4:32).

Well, enough theology. How about some practical advice, Letterman-style:

### The Top Ten Ways to Turn
### Each Other Away from God

10. Be as holy as you can be. Actually, just be a little holier than your spouse, and put him or her down for falling short of your own personal spiritual achievements.

9. Only quote the Bible verses you personally have obeyed.

8. Be the judge and jury—and God.

7. If you know that being judgmental is not Christian, be patronizing and condescending instead.

6. Use God to manipulate and control other people, especially each other.

5. Pretend. Don't ever get real. Unless you need to get real mad because you know how upset God is with your spouse.

4. Do things with a religious tone and a religious air. Work on this when you are in church. Quote the Bible when you know God is on your side.

3. Let your life be fear-driven. And use fear to control your spouse, or at least to get your spouse to do what you want.

2. Let your life be rule-driven. Make rules more important than love.

1. Choke on cigarette smoke, but swallow whole porcupines. Or, make the little things really big things.

---

**AND IN THE LAST CHAPTER ...**

**CAN YOU GET TO HEAVEN**

**WITHOUT FAMILY DEVOTIONS?**

---

TEN

---

## LIVING BY BREAD ALONE

---

*Can you get to heaven without family devotions?*

Family prayer and Bible reading.

Guilt.

I confess. I am better at being a pastor than I am at family devotions.

But then I'm not telling you anything you don't already know, Dave, because you grew up right here in a pastor's home, where formal family Bible studies were few and far between.

So what am I doing writing about family devotions in this book? Who do I think I am?

I'm just one more guy called to the ministry and gifted to speak, but I'm also just one more guy who struggles with the same issues as everyone else in our church.

At least I'm honest.

In spite of my personal failure, though (maybe partly because of it), I think I have some advice on the subject that can help you two—and everyone else reading this book.

### THE DUNGEON OF SILENT GUILT

Before you were married, when you were living with us, Jill, I decided to give a talk in church on family devotions. I dreaded it, Dave, because your mother knew the truth.

LIVING BY BREAD ALONE

But I also knew that most of the husbands and wives in our church suffer the silent guilt of inconsistent family prayer and that, at the very least, they would feel a whole lot better about themselves if they heard that Mom and I struggle with the same issue.

There are, of course, people who really do pray every day with their spouses and children. These are the notable exceptions—fine Christians who are genuinely self-disciplined in their personal devotions. These are good people who really love God, and who *unintentionally* make us feel bad about not praying enough.

Actually, I have to put in a word for your wonderful mom. Whatever ways I failed you kids, she was as faithful as the sunrise in praying with each of you almost every night, just before "lights out." She read Bible stories to you, too, which you may or may not remember.

But devotions with all of us sitting together in the family room, listening attentively to me reading God's Word ... well ... it just didn't happen that often.

At any rate, when I decided to preach a sermon on something I don't do myself (of course, preachers hardly *ever* do that—at least that's what they want you to think), I decided to look for some resources on family prayer time, what to do and how to do it. If I couldn't speak out of my own personal experience, maybe I could tell stories about somebody else.

I visited a gargantuan Christian book outlet store here in Phoenix. Hiking to the huge family book section in the back of the store, I was shocked (but also strangely comforted) to find no books, *zero, zip,* on how to have family devotions. Not one.

"At least I should be able to find a chapter or two on the subject," I muttered to myself.

Among the stacks in front of me was a particularly fat book entitled *The Strong Family*, by no less a light than Charles

Swindoll. "Over 250,000 copies in print," announced the bright blue cover.

"This has to have *something*," I thought. But I was genuinely disappointed. Not a single chapter on family prayer. In fact, the words "devotions" and "prayer" did not even appear in the index!

After skimming the "Table of Contents" page of every other available book on those jammed shelves ... still nothing!

"What am I gonna do?" I agonized. "I've already announced the upcoming sermon to the whole church!"

And then it came to me: Focus on the Family! If anyone would have stuff on family devotions, it would be Focus on the Family. So I had my assistant, Penny Jo, call them.

"We have daily devotional guides," they told her. "But, no, we don't actually have something that explains *how* to have family devotions."

Hello?

Am I missing something?

### HELPLESS IN PHOENIX

Now I know that there must be some Christian books out there about how to do family devotions. And I don't want to suggest for a minute that Charles Swindoll or James Dobson would not be the first to talk about how family prayer is absolutely necessary for a strong family. They are fine, godly men, with outstanding ministries. I love what they do!

But it's amazing to me that a big Christian bookstore, burgeoning with books on the family, did not have a single guide to family prayer!

Is it so simple that no one needs to explain it? That everyone just does it?

Then why is it so hard?

It's easier to sit down and play Monopoly, or put together a jigsaw puzzle, or just sit together watching a mindless TV show, than it is to spend a mere five or ten minutes in prayer together.

Why?

Doesn't "the family that prays together, stay together"?

Maybe we really don't believe that.

We believe eating is important! We always find time to eat. Even when we don't need to eat.

Yet what did Jesus say? "Man does not live on bread alone, but on every word that comes from the mouth of God" (Matthew 4:4).

## THE EXTRAORDINARY POWER OF
## GODLY RELATIONSHIPS

American families have more problems than ever—and less commitment to spiritual things than ever. There's no doubt in my mind that there's a correlation here. *We desperately need God to work in our homes.* The family is a sacred institution. It was God's idea. So David and Jill, you have to keep reminding yourselves of the extraordinary power of the family, both for good and for evil.

It's in the family where we learn about life; about values; about developing relationship skills, like communication, listening, conflict resolution; about love, acceptance, and forgiveness. Most importantly, the family is about cultivating and shaping our relationship with God.

*God works in families!* In fact, I think family is perhaps the single most powerful human institution in the business of life formation—way ahead of the government. And while church is important in life formation, whatever you learn in there—for the smidgen of time each week that you're there—has to be lived out somewhere else. The close relationships of the family are the best place for that to happen.

*God works in families!* Can you believe that there are more than two thousand verses in the Bible that refer to "house" or "household"? Acts 16:31 is especially poignant: "Believe on the Lord Jesus, and you will be saved—you *and your household.*" Nobody goes to heaven because someone else believes. Nothing in the Christian life is automatic, but this verse unveils an awesome spiritual power in the family system.

Alluding to this power in 1 Corinthians 7:12-14, Paul commands, "If you are a man with a wife who is not a believer but who still wants to live with you, hold on to her. If you are a woman with a husband who is not a believer but he wants to live with you, hold on to him. The unbelieving husband shares to an extent in the holiness of his wife, and the unbelieving wife is likewise touched by the holiness of her husband. Otherwise, your children would be left out; as it is, they also are included in the spiritual purposes of God" (*The Message*).

Hey, the family is spiritual, even when you're not talking about spiritual things. Even when it doesn't *feel* spiritual. The family is spiritual because it's sacred. Prayer, even in small doses, releases the full power of God's presence and blessing into your relationship.

John Bunyan, author of the classic *Pilgrim's Progress,* declared, "You can do more than pray after you have prayed. But you cannot do more than pray, until you have prayed."

And Kent and Barbara Hughes, in *Common Sense Parenting,* write, "Certainly, there are many other indispensable elements to Christian parenting, but prayer is of the utmost importance."[1]

Evelyn Christenson, in *What Happens When We Pray for Our Families,* writes, "Prayer should be the spontaneous lifestyle of every Christian family, especially today because the family as the world has known it for centuries is disintegrating before our eyes."[2]

Notice she says that prayer should be "the spontaneous lifestyle." So why isn't it? And how can you make it happen? How do you do it?

## TOO BUSY FOR GOD

As I see it, there are two barriers to overcome. I can tell you about the first one, but I can't do much to help you: *We're too busy.*

In Luke 10:38-42, there's a story about a woman named Martha, who opened her home to Jesus. She had a sister called Mary, who sat at the Lord's feet listening to what he said. But Martha was distracted by all the preparations that had to be made.

"Lord, don't you care that my sister has left me to do the work by myself? Tell her to help me!"

"Martha, Martha," the Lord answered. [Ever have your mother call your name twice?] "You are worried and upset about many things, but only one thing is needed. Mary has chosen what is better, and it will not be taken away from her."

In the Old Testament, Isaiah the prophet says something similar: "This is what the Sovereign Lord, the Holy One of Israel, says, 'In repentance and rest is your salvation, *in quietness and trust is your strength,* but you would have none of it" (Isaiah 30:15). Jesus calls us to himself, but we are too busy to listen and receive.

"Our busy world," observes Kent Hughes, "is inhospitable to prayer, because it neither understands prayer nor allows time for it. We have to fight for prayer time."[3]

Don't we know it! But like I said, I can't do anything to make you unbusy, and it's not just going to happen. You have to *make* time for each other and for God. If you don't, you will pay the price. I heard recently that up to 90 percent of all visits to the family doctor are as a result of stress-related illness.

You know about my heart, Dave. Not good.

And you're only twenty-two, but you've already had to see a doctor about your severe headaches.

David, David. Jill, Jill. You are worried and upset about many things (or troubled and stressed—whatever words suit you). Only one thing is essential, and Mary has chosen it—it's the main course.

### TOO SPIRITUAL FOR DEVOTIONS

And the second barrier to family devotions? This may sound dumb, but *we're too spiritual.* We think of family devotions as a kind of formal religious exercise, and people have crazy ideas—myths—about religious behavior.

Like family devotions have to be *long*, at least a half-hour.

They have to be *deep*, too. If what you talk about isn't worth publishing, it's not deep enough.

They have to be *church-like*. Structured. Stiff. Voice tones just right.

They have to *feel* spiritual. And *you* have to feel spiritual—before, during, and after. If you don't feel a lingering sense of God's presence for at least a little while after the closing prayer, then your devotions were surely a bust.

You have to sing. Even if no one in your family knows how to sing. If you feel self-conscious about singing together, it must be a sign of a deeper sin.

Everybody has to make up their prayers. And they'd better be good—and new and different. You can never read a prayer, because it's a sign of a lack of a real relationship with God.

You also must assume that you are the only couple who struggles with these issues, or that you are the only young couple in the church that doesn't like to sing together.

Kent and Barbara Hughes couldn't say it better: "When Christian couples begin life together, they often share an idealized picture of domestic devotion. They imagine themselves leisurely reading the Bible together, discussing at length a rich devotional thought, praying around the globe, singing together, and dropping off to sleep in each other's arms as their Bible slips to the floor."[4]

## TIPS TO PUT YOU OVER THE TOP

Dave and Jill, when I preached about this at our church, hundreds of families pledged to do devotions for four weeks. I gave them an attainable goal: to commit to family devotions for just four weeks, in the hope that it would enable people to break through the barriers of busyness and religious myth to form new habits of family spirituality.

It even worked for Mom and me! Remember, Jill, you were living in our home while Dave was away in California finishing his college work, and we actually had daily (almost) devotions for a month!

Try it for yourself.

- Keep it real simple.
- Start by tracking your progress on a calendar: any five of seven days a week. Give yourself a grace space twice a week. Hey, five for seven is better than none for seven!
- Each day you pray, mark your calendar with a check, or an "x," or maybe a cross!
- Each day, read one chapter of the Gospel of John from a modern translation or paraphrase, like the *New International Version* (NIV) or the *New Living Bible*, or *The Message*. John has twenty chapters, so you should finish reading it by the end of the four weeks.
- Or pick up a *simple* daily devotional guide from a Christian bookstore. (They have lots of daily guides, just no book on *how* to do it!)

- Decide on something you need to pray about that day and pray a simple prayer. Or pray a written prayer from a devotional guide or prayer book.
- Try to do it the same time each day, like right before breakfast, or right after dinner, or right before bedtime.
- Include the kids when you have 'em. Everyone in your family should come together for your prayer time, and everyone should respect that time as God's time, but don't *force* anyone to pray, especially the kids. Make it easy on yourself and them.
- When you have kids, keep your devotions on the level of your youngest child, which means that reading long portions of the Bible may be too difficult for them. Instead of reading a whole chapter from John, for example, just read five or ten verses. Don't worry if your time together doesn't seem long enough, or spiritual enough. *Just do it!*

Well, it's over.

The book, that is, but not your life. It's easier, Dave and Jill, to read a book—and even agree with most everything in it— than it is to be married! Actually, it's *much* easier.

So where do you go from here? I suggest if a chapter (or two or three) was especially meaningful, that you re-read it, perhaps once a year. I know this is not commonly done, because when you finish a book you stick it away, or pass it on to someone else. But some things need to be said—and read—more than once.

I also suggest that you do two things that have really helped your mother and me: *one*, commit yourself to a small group of close friends and meet *regularly*, no less than once a month. I have become convinced, especially with the demise of the extended family, that couples need support groups where they can talk about everything from family devotions to sex.

The bottom line is accountability. You need people you love and trust who will listen to your pain, give you good counsel, and speak into your life. You might even want to use this book as a discussion guide for your support group meetings.

*Two*, get counseling from a Christian professional when you need it and as soon as you need it. One of the worst things you can do is tell yourself that your problem will just go away, or that a counselor can't tell you anything new. Hey, Mom and I have been married for twenty-five years, and now I'm really an expert because I've written a book on marriage. But off and on, we've had to talk to someone we trusted, someone trained and skilled in the art of family counseling, because you just can't fix yourself. It's the way God made you. You need each other, and you need others.

Finally, I know you are already committed to this, but don't ever let yourself drift away from church. I have a friend, a high-powered corporate executive. I had a couple of seminary classes with him. He loves God, but he hated to go to church. I mean, he just never went. His wife did, and she took the children.

One day, at lunch, I challenged him, "If you don't go to church for any other reason, do it for your family."

He did.

Years later, he keeps thanking me for that advice, even though he still attends a boring church regularly.

Just because you think something is boring, doesn't mean it isn't good for you. The discipline and routine of regular church attendance build character and faithfulness into our lives.

But there's more. We live in a godless world, and going to church keeps us in touch with the few people in our lives who are godly. I didn't say perfect. Nobody's perfect. No, not even the people who stay away from church because the people who go to church aren't perfect.

My friend and colleague of many years, Chris Wolfard, readily admits that he doesn't like to go to church, but when he was out of the ministry for a year or so, he eagerly accepted my invitation to return because, he said, he did not trust himself alone, outside the Christian community. He admitted he needed the structure and the discipline to keep his life on track.

So do you.

So deal with it.

This book is short, like life. Before you know it, you'll be "old" like your mother and me.

Put God first.

Put God first.

Put God first.

## ONE
*Till Death Do Us Part, or For As Long As I'm Happy*

1. Kim Lawton, "'No Fault' Divorce Under Assault," *Christianity Today* (April 8, 1996), 84.
2. *Marriage in America: A Report to the Nation* (New York: Institute for American Values, March 1995), 3,4,5. Copies of the report can be obtained by contacting: Institute for American Values, 1841 Broadway, Suite 211, New York, NY 10023. Tel: (212) 246-3942. Fax: (212) 541-6665.
3. *Marriage in America*, 8.
4. Marvin Wilson, *Our Father Abraham: Hebrew Roots of the Christian Faith* (Grand Rapids, Mich.: Eerdmans, 1989), 207.
5. Wilson, 203.
6. Wilson, 206.

## TWO
*No Sniveling*

1. I am indebted to Doug Murren for the graphic description of life in the First Century in the three paragraphs immediately above, from his book *Is It Real When It Doesn't Work?* , (Nashville:Nelson, 1990), 14.
2. "The Fall and Rise of Marriage," *Christianity Today* (May 15, 1995), 14.

3. Murren, 35.

### THREE
*Good Sex*

1. R. Kent Hughes, *Disciplines of a Godly Man* (Wheaton: Crossway Books, 1991), 23-24.
2. Francine Prose, Erica Jong, Dana Kennedy, Cathy Reiner, "Writing the book on good sex," *The Arizona Republic*, Section AzW, July 28, 1992.
3. As quoted by James J. Kilpatrick, "Our society is sliding downhill: What has caused this abandonment of the old virtues? Much of it can be blamed squarely upon the media," *The Arizona Republic*, August 31, 1991.
4. Marriane K. Hering, "Believe Well, Live Well," *Focus on the Family*, September 1994, 4.
5. Laurie Hall, *An Affair of the Mind* (Colorado Springs: Focus on the Family, 1996), 51.
6. Hall, 110.
7. Hall, 110.
8. Steven Naifeh and Gregory Smith, *Why Can't Men Open Up?* (New York: Clarkson N. Potter, Inc., 1984), 5.
9. As quoted by Reiner, 1.
10. Steven Covey, *Seven Habits of Highly Effective People* (New York: Simon and Schuster, 1989), 240.
11. As quoted by Robert Hicks, *Uneasy Manhood* (Nashville: Oliver Nelson, 1991), 104.

## FOUR
*Why Can't We All Just Get Along?*

1. Paul is speaking here of the hostility between Jews and Gentiles, but the principle of reconciliation breaks down every other imaginable "dividing wall of hostility" too.
2. David Watson, *Called and Committed* (Wheaton, Ill.: Harold Shaw, 1982), 186.
3. Les Parrott III and Leslie Parrott, *Saving Your Marriage Before It Starts* (Grand Rapids: Zondervan, 1995), 16.
4. Parrott, 20.
5. Doug Murren, *Is It Real When It Doesn't Work* (Nashville: Thomas Nelson, 1990), 132.
6. Richard Foster, *Prayer* (San Francisco: HarperCollins, 1992), 62.

## FIVE
*What to Do?*

1. The two preceding paragraphs are from Haddon Robinson, *Decision-Making By the Book* (USA, Canada, England: Victor Books, 1991), 11.
2. M. Blaine Smith, *Knowing God's Will* (Downers Grove, Ill.: InterVarsity, 1991), 27.
3. Robinson, 164.
4. Robinson, 164.
5. Robinson, 164.

## SIX
### *Thank God It's Monday*

1. R. Kent Hughes, *Disciplines of a Godly Man* (Wheaton, Ill: Crossway, 1991) 139.
2. Mike Rogers and Claude King, *The Kingdom Agenda* (Murfreesboro, Tenn.: Kingdom Agenda Ministries, 1996), 22-23.
3. Adapted from Sherman and Hendricks, *Your Work Matters To God* (Colorado Springs: NavPress, 1987).
4. Rogers and King, 96.


## SEVEN
### *Holy Money! Batman*

1. Nancy Gibbs, "Emotional Intelligence," *Time,* October 2, 1995, 60ff.
2. Neale Godfrey and Carolina Edwards, *Money Doesn't Grow on Trees* (New York: Simon & Schuster, 1994), 13-14.
3. Robert Wuthnow, *God and Mammon in America* (New York: Macmillan, 1994), 135.
4. Godfrey and Edwards, 14.
5. Godfrey and Edwards, 52.
6. As reported in the *National and International Religion Report,* February 6, 1995, 4.
7. Jacques Ellul, *Money and Power* (Downers Grove, Ill.: InterVarsity Press, 1984), 113.

## EIGHT
*SuperGlue*

1. Kathleen Farmer, *Who Knows What Is Good* (Grand Rapids, Mich.: Eerdmans, 1991), 26.

## NINE
*How to Be Godly Without Being Obnoxious*

1. Rebecca A. Clay, "Psychologists' Faith in Religion Begins to Grow," *The APA Monitor*, Volume 27: Number 8, August, 1996, 1, 48.
2. Clay, 48.
3. I've merged these two translations in this excerpt. Italics are from J. B. Phillips.

## TEN
*Living By Bread Alone*

1. Evelyn Christenson, *What Happens When We Pray for Our Families* (Wheaten, Ill.: Victor, 1992), **10.** (Whoops. Sounds like this is a book about how to have devotions. Well, it does tell you what happens when you do, but it doesn't have a single a chapter on how to do it.)
2. Kent and Barbara Hughes, *Common Sense Parenting* (Wheaton: Tyndale, 1995), 89.
3. Hughes, 90.

## OTHER BOOKS BY GARY KINNAMAN

### MY COMPANION THROUGH GRIEF
*Comfort for Your Darkest Hours*

"God's future is always one day ahead of our worst day," writes Pastor Gary Kinnaman. Having comforted many families agonizing over the loss of a loved one, the author has drawn from the collective wisdom of great Christian men and women to write a book to help those passing "through the valley of the shadow." *My Companion Through Grief* answers many of the difficult questions people face in their grief: *Why did God allow this to happen? Does he know how much it hurts? Does he care?*

No one can pass through life without being touched by death. This book is for all those who are grieving and who are helping others through their time of loss.

$12.99, TRADE PAPER

### ANGELS DARK AND LIGHT

Angelic encounters seem to be on the rise today. But angels have always been a part of human history, most commonly depicted in the Bible itself.

In *Angel's Dark and Light*, Gary Kinnaman provides a thoroughly biblical guide to the world of angels. He pulls back the curtain on this fascinating supernatural phenomena, exploring the nature and purpose of these heavenly encounters. He includes stories about ordinary people who have experienced angelic visitors.

*Angel's Dark and Light* will strengthen readers' faith in God and inspire them with a deeper vision of his power at work in the universe.

$10.99, TRADE PAPER

AVAILABLE FROM YOUR LOCAL CHRISTIAN BOOKSTORE OR
SERVANT PUBLICATIONS, P.O. BOX 8617, ANN ARBOR, MI 48107
PLEASE INCLUDE PAYMENT PLUS $3.25 PER BOOK
FOR SHIPPING AND HANDLING.